The COVID
Letters
Vol. 1

Spencer M. Collins IV

The COVID Letters© 2020
Written By: Spencer M. Collins IV

A portion of the proceeds will go to COVID relief funds.

Published By: Pen Legacy®
Cover By: Ophelia Jessica of ClayHouse Branding
Edited By: Abigail Summer
Formatting By: U Can Mark My Word Editorial Services

ISBN: 978-1-7357512-6-9

Library of Congress Cataloging – in- Publication Data has been applied for.

PRINTED IN THE UNITED STATES OF AMERICA.

Contents

Dedications

This book is dedicated to the brave men and women who risk their lives every day on the front lines of the Corona Pandemic, and to all the lives lost and those affected. This includes my Auntie Gwyndolyn Steven/Collins & my friend Edward Edzo Andrews. Rest In Paradise till we meet again.

As always and with everything I do, this project is done in the name and memory of my dearly departed father and hero, Spencer Michael Collins III, who we lost two years ago. *HAPPY BIRTHDAY, DADDY!*

Chapter One
The Beginning

"We're Only As Sick As Our Secrets"
(If you live it and survive it,
tell it so it loses its power over you.)

When I first got the idea to write this book, I was awakened from a deep sleep where I had a dream of speaking about it on *The Ellen DeGeneres Show*. In the dream, I talked about my intention to donate proceeds of the book to COVID relief funds, and Ellen, in turn, presented me with a giant check. As I stood to receive it, I was jarred out of my sleep with a fire ignited within me, feeling excited to write down all the details I could remember. The only problem was I couldn't remember anything but the title, *The COVID Letters*. So, I quickly got up and called copywriting agencies to reserve the name as my book title.

The following day, I started making calls, looking for a publishing company while still not knowing what the book would be all about, making it difficult to get someone interested in a half-baked idea. Then, after many questions, much rejection, and dealing with my doubts about becoming an author, I finally came up with a notion. The book would be a collection of letters written to our friends, family, and loved ones who lost their lives to the virus, leaving those of us left behind without the opportunity to say goodbye.

This book contains actual letters written during the pandemic with feedback, concerns, questions, and frustrations about other things that are happening in the wake of this pandemic under the administration of a self-serving narcissist who we call President. Please keep in mind that I am not an expert. Everything written on these pages is based on my personal experiences and opinions. Any facts, such as numbers, statistics, and statements, have been researched and confirmed by several reputable organizations before being stated. With that said, once I decided what this book would be about, my final call was to my frat sister, Charron, who not only applauded the idea but was happy to welcome me into the Pen Legacy Family.

Finally, I was onto something, and it all made sense, mainly because I had been personally affected by the virus when I lost two incredibly significant people in my life. I lost my aunt, Dr. and Reverend Gwendylyn Collins/Stephens, and my high school buddy, Edward "Edzo" Andrews, who was also one of my best friends. I decided to include the letters I wrote to them in this book so that others can use the same healing method to get past the sense of helplessness I felt for not being able to pay my last regards.

Without further ado, let's talk about how it all started. 2020 hasn't been kind. In addition to growing concerns of the coronavirus, we were hit with the death of basketball great and (some would say) legend, Kobe Bryant, his daughter, GiGi, and seven other passengers aboard that private Sikorsky S-76B helicopter that crashed in the hills of Malibu on January 26th. This horrific accident sent waves of grief worldwide as we tried to wrap our minds around this senseless tragedy, and our arms around Vanessa, who lost both the love of her life and her daughter. This unimaginable pain drew crowds from around the world to the Staple Center during what we now know to be one of the worst pandemics in global history--the coronavirus. This could have been the start of many of the infections we have in America today, but we'll never know for sure. I only know the loss of Kobe resonated with each of us in such a personal way that we wanted to be a part of it, especially in the celebration of his life and that of his little girl. We never thought about COVID because we all believed we had nothing to be afraid of at the time. What started as a non-threatening outbreak began claiming the lives of hundreds of thousands of people worldwide and affecting the lives of millions while changing the very fabric of life as we knew it forever.

We first learned of the virus from our president during a briefing in January, when the CDC reported the first case in the United States. Soon after that, #45 referred to the virus as the Kung-Flu and called it a Democratic hoax. Since that announcement, the "hoax" up to this point has claimed more than 100,000 lives and has more than 3 million reported cases in the United States alone.

When following the timeline, we've learned that an outbreak began in China back in December of 2019 when many patients were treated for pneumonia and upper respiratory infections. Then, on January 7th and 8th, the CDC started making plans for testing. On the 11th of the same month, the first known death of a 61-year-old man was confirmed in China, and the first known case was reported in the United States. A man traveling from China to Seattle tested positive, and we all watched the spread of this disease become a regular daily conversation as the Trump Administration prepared for its first questions about the virus. In his statement, he announced that he wasn't worried: "No, not at all. We have it all under control. There's one person coming in from China... It's going to be just fine." Right then, I knew we were going to be in trouble, because all I could see was the man who threw toilet paper and paper towels to victims suffering in Puerto Rico after Hurricane Maria left the state devastated in October of 2017.

More than 200 people lost their lives to the virus during this time, and almost 10,000 had already been infected. Being led to believe this was no great concern for the United States, many of us let our guards down and did not take the proper precautions to protect ourselves and others, which later proved devastating as the virus quickly spread. I remember being slightly alarmed as a person who lives with a pre-existing medical condition, likes to travel, and has a family that lives 2,800 miles away in Roslindale, Massachusetts. What would this mean for our travels, upcoming getaways, and family vacations? As life continued across the globe, we held onto the idea of still traveling and vacationing.

Suddenly, it all changed as the impact of this virus was felt worldwide, and cruise ships were prohibited from docking, which led to many losing their lives onboard and others quarantined with hundreds of infected passengers. Europe and Italy saw sudden surges in new cases, and we were now in a full-fledged panic as new infections began to show up worldwide.

I remember being sick during this time. I wasn't able to catch my breath, experienced headaches, night sweats, dizzy spells, nausea, and anxiety attacks. I also remember my close circle of friends feeling the same way. However, most felt better within a few days. Unfortunately, I did not.

After a couple of weeks, I became genuinely concerned, mostly because of the multiple news reports. Even though earlier reports seemed to suggest that African Americans were somehow immune to the virus, I never considered it to be true. I spent the next few weeks running back and forth to the emergency room, trying to figure out what was going on in my body. I even quarantined myself and walked away from several projects, fearing I may have been exposed to the virus and not wanting to risk exposing others.

On lockdown for three weeks, I was going crazy listening to the news and concerns that this virus was growing out of control. For the latter part of January and February, I spent most of my time trying to get tested, going to my primary care physician, the ER, and even urgent care, seeking testing for COVID-19. It wasn't until a visit in early March that I was informed testing was reserved only for those working on the front lines. So, I was sent home to treat my symptoms and advised that if I got worse, I should come back to the same place that never told me why they couldn't test me in the first place.

As you can imagine, this didn't make me feel safe or have any trust in the healthcare system, which only triggered my anxiety. For those that deal with this condition, you know once triggered, the floodgates are now open, and it becomes difficult to manage, especially if you're still dealing with what started it. I also have asthma and CHF (Congestive Heart Failure). These medical issues only exacerbated my other conditions, leaving me drained completely. Not to mention having to handle being flooded with all the constant news reports and endless changing information about the virus, its symptoms, who it infects, how it's transmitted, and who is at risk. I was a basket case trying to keep up with all the information, doing my best not to panic or take on too much of what was said.

The thing I remember most about this time is how nonchalant some of the care providers in our community were, especially for the fact that most of us had pre-existing medical conditions. I know they didn't have many facts about the virus yet, but I also knew they were a lot more cautious in areas outside of the African American community. As the threat continued to grow and #45 still insisted we were okay, on January 30th, the WHO declared the outbreak to be a "public health emergency of international concern." This was enough to raise eyebrows, as we were finally getting more details about this mysterious and deadly virus. Still, I can't help but wonder if it's a hoax or if it is real. But considering contradicting reports and fake news circulating daily, the only thing that's sure is that some form of this virus does exist. Still suffering from flu-like symptoms, I wondered if I would be another statistic, or would we get ahead of this thing and finally not be left in the dust by other countries dealing with the same threat? I've watched every news report, press conference, and have even done my own research, and all of it looks bad.

On January 31st, the United States followed the

WHO's lead and declared a public health emergency that triggered "Emergency Use Authorization." This action sounded good to most of us that didn't have a general knowledge of these types of policies and procedures. Being that I was at home doing nothing, I had time to research and discover that this policy discouraged labs from doing in-home testing because approval from the FDA is required.

Now I don't know about you, but whenever I hear that the FDA is involved in anything, it makes me nervous. How can you trust the Food and Drug Administration that has approved several products whose side effects are worse, or in many cases just as bad, as the illness or disease being treated? Westernized medicine and pharmaceutical companies' main objective is to get paid for their services and medications provided. They are not concerned with saving lives, just extending them long enough for patients to be treated with medications that make them a fortune.

As many friends and family began losing jobs, closing their businesses, and applying for unemployment benefits, it became painfully apparent that things would get worse before they got better. The stock market crashed, folks scrambled to figure out what to do with their finances, and savings depleted as folks were left trying to figure out how to survive while struggling to pay rent and feed their families. As an answer to people's growing concern about not having money or food, a stimulus package was created. Although I never received mine nor did millions of other Americans, many others did, but was it enough for those out of work for weeks and even months to catch up?

The answer is no, even though the $1,200 per individual, $1,200 per head of household, $2,400 per couple, and $500 per child was better than nothing. These allocated funds still weren't enough to catch up on overdue rent, pay current and past-due bills, and put food on the table. So, families still had to make choices that would leave them without these things and more. In the meantime, black men were still being gunned down in the streets, hunted by the police and "concerned citizens" who were encouraged by #45's silence during protests as he reignited race wars with antisemitism tweets and comments. So, while the rest of the world is worrying about fighting the virus, we, as African Americans, are fighting for justice and our lives, just as it has always been the case.

As we prepared to take to the streets in protest while the number of infections continued to rise, we noticed an all-too-familiar trend; the Black and Brown communities are being disproportionately affected once again. In the past, a pandemic may have kept us from doing what needed to be done, but not this time. Folks of all colors and races grabbed their masks, signs, and bullhorns and took to the streets. Friends, families, and coworkers showed up in the streets worldwide, protesting about their dissatisfaction. The risk of being exposed was not greater than the cause of not getting involved to make and force a change.

With everything going on in the world, I wondered how I could contribute to this historical moment without putting my life at risk because of my pre-existing health conditions. It later came to me that many before me had risked their lives with pre-existing conditions of hatred, bigotry, and racism, but that didn't stop them from making their contributions and being heard. First, I decided to write a letter to focus and keep my thoughts from consuming me and getting caught up in the emotions. Being a black man in America, as you can imagine, has been very traumatizing, starting with the circumstances of our very violent history leading up to our very violent existence now. When the opportunity presented itself for me to be a part of the first Black Lives Matter movement in solidarity with the LGBTQI community, I knew it was a sign to get involved, and I just did it!

Dear Self,

I know these are scary times, and with everything going on, you don't want to expose yourself to the virus unnecessarily. Have you ever considered that being a part of the Black Lives Matter collective body and movement is indeed necessary to ignite a fire that could spark that change? Have you also considered the hundreds and thousands of ancestors that sacrificed their lives so you could live yours, and what a bold and selfless testament you'd be making to their stand for you to be a part of this movement?

Might I also remind you that like He has brought you through before, He can and will do it again if it is His will. This life that you're living is not your own, and as you've witnessed time and time before, you and everyone here is on borrowed time. When that clock stops ticking, whether you're at home alone or in a crowd surrounded by people, your time is up. So, you have the choice of staying at home in bed being a victim or getting up and being one of the many heroes you often read about. It's your choice. Just remember that without sacrifice, there is no change.

Faith is not believing, "I can do some things through Jesus Christ," but instead, "I can do ALL things through Jesus Christ who strengthens me."

Of course, in all thy getting, first, gain an understanding. You can't go into any war without armor and weapons. In this case, the armor is the mask, gloves, and hand sanitizer, and your weapon is His word and promise.

Ephesians 6:10-20 – Finally be strong in the Lord and in his

mighty power. Put on the full armor of God, so that you can take your stand against the devil's schemes. For our struggle is not against flesh and blood, but against the rulers, against the authorities, against the powers of this dark world and against the spiritual forces of evil in the heavenly realms. Therefore, put on the full armor of God, so that when the day of evil comes, you may be able to stand your ground, and after you have done everything, to stand. Stand firm then, with the truth buckled around your waist, with the breastplate of righteousness in place, and with your feet fitted with the readiness that comes from the gospel of peace. In addition to all this, take up the shield of faith, with which you can extinguish all the flaming arrows of the evil one. Take the helmet of salvation and the sword of the Spirit, which is the word of God.

And pray in the spirit on all occasions with all kinds of prayers and requests. With this in mind, be alert and always keep on praying for all the Lord's people. Pray also for me, that whenever I speak, words may be given me so that I will fearlessly make known the mystery of the gospel, for which I am an ambassador in chains. Pray that I may declare it bold and fearlessly, as I should.

Never forget whose you are and where you come from. God didn't bring you this far to leave you, and if He gives you the mind and desire to do something, follow His plan because He's already proven to you what He can and will do.

From the Believer in You,
Cer Collins (Son Of Billie Jean)

Chapter Two
Self-Quarantine

This month has been crazy. I've already been to the hospital, emergency room, and doctors several times, and I still haven't been tested for COVID. This is particularly scary because of the warnings we keep hearing on TV just about every day.

To catch you up to speed, on February 4th, the CDC shipped out 200-plus test kits nationwide and informed the labs of them the following day. Meanwhile, the WHO had shipped out 250,000 kits. These new tests were supposed to go to those high risk on the front line, the elderly, and those with pre-existing conditions. However, one had still not been made available to me. So, while they were telling us one thing on television, it was something completely different in reality. Welcome to the great United States of America!

As a black man living with HIV, I am often treated as a number, but as a black man living with HIV in an urban community, I've gotten used to being treated as even less than that. It's no secret that we are not afforded the same level of treatment or have access to the same resources found in wealthy communities, but it is something we don't talk about enough. Mostly because it makes folks feel uncomfortable. The other reason is that some people have no idea what goes on outside of their communities. So, they assume everything is okay or that we're not well because we choose not to be.

Poverty is not a choice. It's a lifestyle forced upon those that don't make enough income to be considered middle-class, thereby making them poor. One of the most expensive states in America besides New York is California, where almost 40 million other people and I reside. On average, a low budget, basic lifestyle is between $40-45K, which means you'd need to be making $50K plus a year. As an unemployed, disabled person who has Medi-Medi (Medicare and Medicaid), I can tell you personally that it's not a choice. There are many places I would like to go for treatment, and although it is assumed I can go to any of those places, the truth is I cannot. When you go to a medical facility, the first question they ask is: Do you have your ID and insurance card? This often sets the tone for how you'll be treated, not to mention your skin color. I know we would all like to believe this is not the case, but I can assure you that it most certainly is.

Most of my appointments are through the AHF (AIDS Healthcare Foundation). When I'm there, the medical staff is so concerned with my HIV status that they often overlook my other health concerns or do not address them. Unfortunately, a person kind of gets used to it, especially if you are a black patient. So, when they weren't doing anything to address the fact that I was having symptoms synonymous with the coronavirus, I wasn't surprised but disappointed as usual. I even went to other hospitals hoping the treatment would be different, but after I arrived, what often stood out to me was the condition of the places, the number of people waiting to be seen, and the long wait times. I was frightened every time I had to be in the presence of others who seemed to be sick, too, but didn't have on masks and weren't separated or being managed like they were a potential threat. So, after being sent home multiple times without being tested, I blended back into my routine without any treatment or medications, believing I was okay to do so. I mean, that's what the doctors said, and we all trust our doctors, right? Yeah, that's what I thought, too! Only for many reasons, I don't!

Anyway, it was back to work for me, and although I wasn't feeling my best, my village and I had a major audition for an opportunity to be in a national commercial, and I wasn't about to mess that up for any of us. So, I went home to rest up. My partner gave me some home remedies, Dr. Sholtz and his special healing concoctions, and I rested until it was time to show up and perform. My crew knew I wasn't feeling well, but they also knew I would do anything for them just as they would for me. So, while they brought fruit, liquids, homemade soups, and love, I returned the favor by bringing them me.

There is nothing like being surrounded by people that love you to make you feel better. So, we headed out and had an amazing time doing what we do best--having a good time and enjoying each other's company, only this time in a room full of directors, agents, and producers. Afterward, we went to the Cheesecake Factory to celebrate. While breaking bread, sharing food, and toasting with drinks, we were also potentially passing germs we didn't even know we had. You see, this is the damage that was done for hundreds of thousands, maybe even millions, around the world when we were told by #45 that "Kung-Flu" wasn't serious. How can you protect yourself from a threat you don't know exists?

In the days that followed, I remember talking to everyone and getting the news that they weren't feeling well. They all complained of the same symptoms: headache, nausea, nasal congestion, night sweats, and diarrhea. Of course, at the time, we all believed we had a seasonal bug or virus, or maybe the food from our celebration made us sick. We never even considered it could be COVID-19. Quite frankly, we can't prove now that it was or wasn't, only that the symptoms were coincidentally the same. Looking back, I now believe we were all exposed to the virus that day or maybe sooner, maybe even by me.

I also believe many Americans had already been exposed and didn't know because our administration failed to warn us. Do I have proof? No, only the corrupt behavior of this country's history as an example of some of the wicked things they are willing to do to hide the truth about who they are and what they are capable of doing. I won't bore you with all the sordid details, but let's mention a couple in case you have any doubts.

For instance, when Christopher Columbus, who so-called discovered America (a land already populated with Native Americans), brought smallpox, measles, and influenza to North America, killing an estimated 2-18 million and shrinking the population down to about 530,000 by the end of the 19th century. Or how about in 1932 when they purposely infected almost 400 black men with syphilis during a 600-patient study that was supposed to last six months, but instead, it went on for 40 years.

I would go on, but it isn't necessary. I'm sure if you dig into the history of our country, you'll discover for yourself the skeletons buried beneath its stories and lies. Therefore, many people believe this is some conspiracy, and that the United States, along with other countries, are using it as a form of population control for a new genocide to reduce the already overpopulated globe. I don't know what I think anymore, just that I'm afraid I may pass whatever it is I have to others, which is not what I want.

Two days before filming on February 12th, they announced some trouble with testing kits (states had inconclusive lab results). Oh, yeah, did I mention we got the job? When I say "we", I'm referring to my crew-- Apollo, Donnie, Gego, Jessica, and Pia. Pia had just returned from Thailand, which is not too far from where the outbreak began in China. We were all super excited to have her there, although I must admit that we probably would've needed a stand-in if this happened now. Don't get me wrong, we love our girl, but ain't nobody tryna get sick. They almost didn't let her Momma Day back over here, but our circle is protected. So, by God's good grace, they beat the cutoff and were released back to us.

On February 14th, the same day we filmed, the U.S. confirmed 15 cases here in the states. Most were travelers from Wuhan. I remember thinking, "Wasn't Pia's ass near there? Uhhh-uhhh, I betta stay away from her." But, as she got out of the car, I was probably the first to grab and hug her. Not that I wasn't scared; just that I love her so much it didn't matter. Plus, I had no real idea of how the virus was transmitted, and neither did the rest of the world. At least that's what we believed at the time.

We briefly joked while on set but had to be careful about what we said since we were mic'd up and under surveillance. It was so cold that day. I remember thinking even if Pia did have it, we weren't in danger of catching it. From what I heard, the virus can't survive in extreme cold or heat, isn't passed through the air, and isn't that contagious, especially amongst blacks. So, we're good! Having no accurate information about how the virus spreads, we went on the rest of the night laughing, sharing food, breathing in each other's faces, and spreading respiratory droplets while spending Love Day together as friends and getting paid to do so.

The following week, February 23rd, we got the official word from Timothy Stenzel of the FDA that there was a problem with the CDC's instructions concerning testing. What the problem was we'll probably never know because, like most things, they partially share information with the public. But, despite whatever it was, life goes on, and we had one more day of shooting to complete. Again, there still hadn't been a real sense of urgency established by our leaders during this time. So, most of the country carried on as though it were just another day. No social distancing, no masks. Only the knowledge of some Chinese flu that was thousands of miles away from us. Meanwhile, we were still sharing food, drinks, hugs, kisses, and other things we're no longer allowed to do.

After we wrapped, I went home and promised my partner that I would slow down as I was still dealing with the symptoms from this mysterious infection that my doctor refused to treat. Still wheezing, congested, and having a small fever, I decided to pull out of the projects I was currently working on and quarantined myself until we figured out exactly what was going on with me.

The first few days weren't too bad; breakfast in bed, body rubs, foot detoxes, and lots of attention from the very sweet and handsome mista. I mean, what more could a gay man or straight woman ask for? I was in heaven. Then the breathing, the sweats, the fever, and discomfort got worse. While sitting and watching the news, I went into panic mode, getting conflicting and contradicting information from the president and the Rona task force.

My anxiety level increased, and with it came a familiar feeling of darkness, one I had experienced before but didn't quite know how to deal with or describe. It made me unable to focus, sleep, and enjoy things that had normally given me great pleasure. Yes, I'm talking about the D-Word. The word most African Americans have a hard time discussing. DEPRESSION! Though it was something I've dealt with before, it was different this time. Mostly because before, I would throw myself into my work to help cure me, but this time, all my outlets had been stifled by the fact that I wasn't going out. Being a social butterfly and workaholic, I wasn't sure how to get past this moment. While others suggested being creative and doing some things and projects I've always wanted to do, my depression kept me from being focused long enough to accomplish doing them. Not that I didn't try, because I did. I started six different projects but couldn't finish any of them. As I mentioned in chapter one, the news reports and press releases consumed me, and none of them added anything but more anxiety to my day.

Staying at home became more of a sacrifice than I imagined. Not only was I protecting those around me, but I was dealing with a history of depression that I wasn't ready to acknowledge. I also wasn't doing the homework needed to keep me from entering that space again. Most people think depression is a moment, but it's more than that. These feelings come and go, and you have to do daily maintenance to keep them suppressed. It means dealing with them first and then understanding why they resurface and what triggers it to happen. Sometimes it can be managed without medication, but oftentimes, a licensed therapist has to help you figure out your best treatment, even if it includes a prescribed cocktail.

Fortunately, it was determined early on in my diagnosis, and I learned to open up and be more vocal in expressing my feelings. I no longer held on to my emotions or the secrets that fester and cause emotional distress. So, I started journaling and having open discussions and debates with people who challenged me and who I was becoming, even family members. In this, I found a freedom that allowed me to be me (all of me).

I know it may seem like my thoughts are scattered, and they are. But it's important you understand where my mental state was while dealing with all of this, as I'm certain someone reading this book may be in the same space. It's okay to be in that space, but what's not okay is to stay there. I hope this gives you the permission needed to talk about, write about, pray about, and, most importantly, do something about it. Speaking with Dr. Gloria Morrow helped me get to a space where I was okay with being at home alone with my thoughts. Journaling and composing these letters saved my life.

Speaking of letters, on February 26th, the FDA commissioner sent a letter to the Coalition of Public Health Labs seeking permission to make tests: "False diagnostic test results can lead to significant adverse public health consequences—not only serious implications for individual patient care but also serious implications for the analysis of disease progression and public health decision making." What I understood that to mean was that they didn't want to talk about the negative test but the positive, as that would paint a better picture of what we are dealing with as opposed to what #45 painted the image to be, which meant it's time to be concerned.

On February 29th, the CDC announced the death of a U.S. citizen in his 50s from the state of Washington and the testing of almost 4,000 people nationwide. Also, the FDA then announced a policy that will now make it easier for hospitals to develop their own tests. Though it was painfully obvious that our president-elect still had no clear vision or instructions of what we should be doing, the task force tried to offer suggestions, even while #45 seemed opposed to most of what was being offered. It was at this point that I decided to write this letter:

Dear Mr. President,

I'm not sure what the hell is going on right now. Only that, like most Americans, my concern with this virus is growing as we listen to contradicting hypotheses of what it may be, how it spreads, and its origin. Instead of looking for someone to blame, it might be more productive to utilize our efforts to come up with a plan that will protect our nation and those who are high risk, like our elderly, the front-liners, and those living with preexisting conditions.

I understand that we may not be much of a priority to you, especially with your attempts to end Obamacare, which benefits those living with such medical conditions. I also understand with the changes you wish to make to SSDI, a system that this community of elders and people in need paid into (many before you were even born), that this may disrupt your intentions to strip millions from their disability benefits and sole sources of income. I ask that you have mercy and show compassion and respect for those who have contributed to this already sometimes burdensome system that, for many, is the only resource they have available to assist with their financial and medical needs. Instead of using an already flawed process to harm an already disenfranchised group of suffering elderly, the disabled, and innocent children, I ask that you create ways to protect and further assist them in their time of need. This is your chance to show America you're not the screw-up most of us know you are. It's your opportunity to make up for some of the horrific decisions you've made thus far and truly "Make America Great". Not again, but for the first time. We need you

29

to be our leader and take control of this situation, giving us the marching orders necessary to move past this crisis with grace, poise, and the tools needed for everyone's protection.

Though you have proven during several crises that you are not this person, many of us still pray you will show yourself to be someone new and redeem yourself in many American's eyes that have already given up. This is an opportunity to be the HOPE that Obama left behind.

Take this opportunity to be the man, the president that millions voted to elect as our nation's protector.

Concerned Citizen & Democrat,
Spencer M. Collins IV

Chapter Three
Stay-at-Home Mandate

Finally, I think I'm almost ready to return to work. Hopefully, this virus (whatever it is) will be out of my system in just a couple more days.

January and February had some tough times, and it didn't seem like things could get any worse. However, ever since Rona entered our lives, nothing was the same, and bad days became worse with the news of the virus spreading.

On March 1st, a woman in her late 30s was the next person diagnosed with the coronavirus after traveling to Iran. Five days later, Trump traveled to the CDC wearing a M.A.G.A. hat and reported that tests were complete and nearly perfect, saying, "Anybody who wants a test will get a test." On March 10th, I received a message inviting me to get tested, but I was a lot better at that time. Above all, the thought of going to get tested frightened me. There had been many reports about these tests, and there had been much talk about it amongst us, too. Not to mention the fact that I had been trying to get one for the past two months, and suddenly, now that I could, I didn't trust it.

The following day, one of my favorite Hollywood couples, Rita Wilson and Tom Hanks, announced that they had tested positive for the coronavirus. You know it's serious when celebrities start getting it. They seemed to be okay and in good spirits, though. They even took the time to do interviews, talking about their experience and symptoms since being diagnosed. I'm just glad they're okay. I had the pleasure of meeting and working with them both, and they are the sweetest folks you'll ever meet.

The WHO then declared the coronavirus a pandemic. Also, Redfield reported that the malfunctions occurring with testing kits were probably caused by "a li" or "biologic" factor. I don't know what that is, but it looks like a LIE to me, which further compelled me not to get tested. He followed his findings with a cryptic comment that made me even more uncomfortable: "This is currently under investigation at this point, and I think I'm going to leave it there." What in the hell does that mean, and why does it seem like suddenly everyone is talking in code? Is it because I don't understand half of what they're saying, or is it that fear and anxiety have clouded my mind so much that I can't think straight? Or is it that they *are* talking in code? Either way, this shit is getting out of hand.

To further complicate things and raise red flags, Dr. Fauci, who is part of the task force, testified to Congress and on national television that, "The system is not really geared to what we need right now." He even went on to say, "YES, it's a failure. Let's admit it."

None of this made it any easier for us to do anything that came out of the White House briefings, especially with all the corruption that has already taken place within this administration. Where was Obama when we needed him? I wanted some soothing words of encouragement from someone who knows how to address the reports and the nation without cussing anyone out like #45. This dude acts like he's still on a reality TV show and that this is all some game. It's disturbing to watch as he still hands out pink slips like it's 2008 and we're in the middle of Season 4 of *The Apprentice.* I mean, who actually thought this obnoxious, narcissistic loudmouth would make a good president when he didn't even make a good businessman? He's had six bankruptcies due to over-leveraging hotels and casino businesses in Atlantic City and New York City. He had a failed airline that he had to surrender to his creditors, and on top of it all, he has a long history of racism starting from 1970-2020. He has also made racist, defamatory, and bigoted comments about Muslims, Mexicans, and Blacks. He has even referred to this virus as the "Kung Flu," which is a direct attack on the Asian community. Not to mention personal attacks during his press conferences and the discrimination lawsuits filed against him in the 1970s. So, again, I ask who in the hell thought it was a good idea to make him one of the most powerful people in the world? I'll be the first to admit that, even given his sordid history, I found him quite entertaining on television. However, as a president, he is a stain on America's history and a joke to other world leaders. He is only tolerated because of his title, and even with that, he had to take in some of these mentioned in small doses before they become annoyed and ship him back to his White House.

Now that I got that all out, the same man who told us back in January that we had nothing to worry about and that all was under control now declared this pandemic a national emergency. He even claimed that he knew all along that this would become a pandemic, although we have footage of him stating otherwise. With him, the only reality that exists is the one he creates every time he opens his lying mouth. This is who millions of voters elected to be the 45th President of the United States.

While #45 twiddled his tiny thumbs trying to figure out what the next move should be, mayors and governors were issuing their own orders. Our very own Mayor Eric Garcetti issued a stay-at-home order on March 12th, extending my lockdown indefinitely. I can't say I was happy, but I was relieved to see we were no longer waiting for our president to dictate what we needed to do to make ourselves safe.

As spring break approached, the conversation continued about the stay-at-home orders, and many wondered if it would be enough to stop college crowds from congregating and further spreading this growing virus. Mardi Gras had already quickened the spread of the virus. Even with that knowledge, people were still having large gatherings, parties, and attending events outside of the recommended guidelines. In February, there were no specific guidelines. However, there was a general warning to keep at least a six-feet distance from others until we figured out exactly what this virus was all about. Unfortunately, it was never recommended to cancel events, but people were warned that they should be careful. These are the same people who would be engaging in highly-dangerous activities, rendering them unable to make coherent decisions to protect themselves. Even after the CDC reports suggested that New Orleans had been the perfect breeding ground for the virus and warned that community transmission in these jurisdictions would be high, it wasn't enough to cancel the event. Now, this gathering in Florida would be the same or even more devastating. It seemed like we weren't taking this threat seriously, as people were willing to risk their lives to have a good time. Just as many of us believed this pandemic was real, there was an equal amount who thought it was only a big hoax. Even with the warnings, spring break was still scheduled to happen.

On March 13th, a national emergency was declared,

and life has not been the same since, as the CDC recommended that we were no longer allowed to congregate in groups larger than fifty people. This triggered many states to issue stay-at-home orders, suggesting we all stay home unless we were essential workers. Fear grew as concerts, plays, sporting events, parties, the Olympics, and more were canceled.

With infections rapidly multiplying in the United States, so was the need for more accurate testing. Quicker and more precise testing was needed, and though I was afraid to do so, I knew I needed to find out my status. The talk of the new testing was on everyone's agenda, and people wanted to get their results as soon as possible. Then, on March 27th, it all became possible. Federal health officials gave the green light for a coronavirus test to be provided at point of care, and the results received in less than fifteen minutes using the same technology that powers rapid flu tests. I remember that date because it was my sister Rovenia's birthday, and COVID kept us from celebrating her the way she deserved. Everything was happening so fast, and it felt like the days were blending together.

On March 28th, I mustered up the courage to go and get tested. However, the process was a little overwhelming. I started by logging on to a testing site, finding a location, scheduling a timeslot, printing the receipt, and showing up on the appointed day 10-15 minutes early with a photo ID and the appointment slip. Once we arrived at the site, there was a long line of cars and about 10-12 official city workers, officers, firemen, EMTs, and testers strategically placed in the parking lot to collect our information and move us forward. It looked like a scene from some Sci-fi movie. After waiting forty minutes, it was finally my turn, and they handed me the package with the vile and unopened swab. Then, they gave me instructions on how to self-administer the COVID test. At first, I was a little hesitant to do it; I wanted to trash the kit and speed off. I was so afraid they were going to infect me. But, when I pulled up, one of the officers had lowered his mask and smiled at me. There was something about the warmth of his beautiful smile that made me feel safe. It was as if he was saying, "It's okay. It's all good." So, I followed the instructions, dropped it in the lab bucket, and pulled off to go home and rest.

I was relieved, nervous, anxious, and restless, wondering if I had done the right thing. When would the test be completed? Did they infect me? Would the test be accurate? Is the test real? Was I already sick? For those who have anxiety or are hypochondriacs, you know exactly what I'm talking about. That very moment you can't be still because you believe you already got it. Then, your mind and body begin to create every symptom associated with said illness. Suddenly, you can't breathe, your throat becomes tight, and you feel dizzy and nauseous all at the same time. It was the kind of feeling and situation I was in, but thank God for my partner. His voice soothes me, his hands comfort me, and his chest pressing against mine as he embraces me in a hug makes me feel safe. If that wasn't enough, he would make me a cup of tea and rub my feet until I dozed off. Talk about a chill pill; he is the ultimate serenity.

Before I drifted off to sleep, the last thing I saw was his beautiful, sexy, masculine face with love, concern, and worry that he tried to hide in his eyes. When I woke up to start a new day, I was blessed to see the same again. I must have done something right to have this king in my life, but the question is, what did he do wrong to get me in this? During this lockdown, many of us made discoveries about ourselves, our friends, our families, and our partners/significant others. Don't be afraid of those discoveries! There is nothing wrong with change. Nothing is meant to stay the same, including our relationships as we grow as individuals. We must learn to grow with our family, friends, partners, or lovers.

The term "outgrowing" each other simply means that while one of you is growing, changing, evolving, and transforming, the other is not, and there could be many reasons why that's not happening. This is the right time to find out what those reasons are. As we are all forced to spend more time with each other than we're used to, start asking questions, engaging in healthy debates, and doing what we should have been doing all along. Here's a lil' something to get you started:

- Do they not want to change or grow? If not, why don't they want to change?
- Are you not communicating with each other? If

not, what stops you from doing that, and why?

- Do you still love each other?
- Is love enough? If not, what is?
- Do you still want to be there? If not, where do you want to be?
- Are you happy? If not, what will make you happy?

These questions are not just for you but for all of us going through some difficult times. The questions are to open dialog so that you both can have conversations that let you know where you are and where you're not as individuals, friends, partners, roommates, couples, or whatever the circumstances.

Spencer M. Collins IV

Dear Reader,

I know it sucks being home all the time, but it is important for you and others to comply with these requests, especially while we are trying to figure out this whole pandemic thing. Unfortunately, we still don't know enough about this virus and its behaviors to determine exactly how it is transmitted.

As I watch television and what's happening in other states, I'm frightened to see so many people still partying and carrying on with events that perpetuate the virus's spread with large crowds and gatherings. Until we figure it out, everyone must play a role in promoting and practicing social distancing during these upcoming summer months. This includes everyday preventative measures put in place, such as washing your hands, wearing a mask, avoiding touching your face, and remaining two arm-lengths away from each other. It's really not that hard. Just put on a damn mask and keep your ass at home! Remember, the life you save may be your own or a loved one's.

Follow this simple rule when traveling outside of your home: "Know before you go." Be familiar with local public health authorities' guidelines in the area you're visiting, stores, malls, restaurants, hospitals, hotels, or wherever.

Also, as I mentioned, use this time to check on and communicate with others. Ask questions, pay attention, and talk, talk, talk. Communication is more important than ever during this time. Check on yourself. It's okay to say you are NOT okay, need help, feel alone, or whatever else is on your mind.

You are not in this alone, so don't feel like you have to deal with it by yourself when you're feeling overwhelmed, and reach out for help. I know this is easier said than done since most of us are used to dealing with our issues alone, but now is not the time to take on too much. We already have more than our share of drama to deal with on our own. Don't make Miss Rona one of them.

A Concerned Friend,
Spencer M Collins IV

P.S. - While I'm talking to you, I'm speaking to myself, as well. We got this!

Chapter Four

Saying Goodbye

On March 30th, I woke up to an unusual amount of missed calls and text messages. At first, I was calm, but as I started checking the texts and names of the people who called, I knew right away something was wrong. My heart dropped to my knees. Before returning the calls, I tried to prepare myself for whatever it is they wanted to share. As I looked over the phones numbers, I realized one of the missed calls was from my mother. I became even more reluctant to call back then, because the last time this happened, she was calling to tell me that my daddy had passed. But I took a deep breath and called her anyway, saying hello when she answered.

Right away, she started off the conversation with, "I wanted you to hear this from me first before you hear or see it somewhere else." Then she asked, "Have you talked to your cousin Nikki?'

I knew whatever she was going to tell me would involve the family, but I never thought it would be about Auntie Gwyn.

"Your aunt is gone," she then said. "You should call and check on Nichelle."

I didn't have much of a reaction at the time, but I remember experiencing numbness and guilt about not feeling something more due to the fact that I was in shock. Although Auntie Gwyn had been sick, I wasn't expecting that call and the sad news that came with it.

Finding my voice, I asked my mother if she was alright and told her that I would call Nikki right away. After hanging up, I took a deep breath before calling my cousins. One by one, I got their voicemails until finally, my cousin Mark answered. I talked to him for a little while, expressing my condolences, and then asked to speak to the rest of my cousins. I know what it's like to lose a parent, and I wouldn't wish that unimaginable heart-wrenching pain on my worst enemy. So, when it's someone you love, you can imagine how devastated you will feel.

I stayed on the phone until I spoke to everyone who was capable of speaking, and whoever I did not speak with, I left them a personalized voicemail message. Losing anyone right now is especially painful because it means we won't have an opportunity to say goodbye. So, even though they may not have passed from COVID, their passing is still impacted by the virus.

Shortly after losing my aunt on April 4th, I got the news that an old friend had passed with the virus. I wanted to include them in this book, but the family was too devastated by their passing and requested that I not mention her name. In respecting their wishes, I removed her name along with the letter I had written in her honor. This has been such a traumatic experience for us all, and the last thing I want to do is make it any harder.

Five days later on April 9th, I learned about the passing of another friend, one of my high school besties, Edward "Edzo" Andrews. He did not succumb from COVID but had suddenly passed away after a brief illness. I believe his death could be traced to his broken heart after tragically losing his son. I'm no doctor, though. Just a good friend who witnessed the effect it had on him.

Edzo and I attended Madison Park together, and he was like a big brother to me. He always made sure I was taken care of, especially for the fact that I was still the size of a middle-schooler and greener than a new hundred-dollar bill. He often referred to me as Lil' Huxtable Kid due to my preppy style and the fact that my parents were still together, both had great jobs, and we lived in a pretty decent suburban area at the time. (Not to mention I may have been a little spoiled as a kid.) However, none of that mattered to him. We just enjoyed each other's company and had a lot more in common than not. Even though Edzo lived on what others would call "the other side of the tracks", Grove Hill off Blue Hill Avenue in the

Roxbury area, he was a little spoiled, too! His mother was a hardworking Christian woman like my mom. I don't remember the physical presence of his dad, although I felt like his father--or at least the influence of him--was still around.

We met in Barbra Clancy's class at the Hubert Humphrey Vocational Center in Roxbury, MA, and were studying to be graphic artists. We both loved comic books and Dudley Station hoagies, or subs for you non-East-Coasters! We spent a lot of our time and money on steak & cheese or Italian subs. Then we would go to Skippy Whites to buy the latest Ca Singles. Don't act like you don't remember what those. You know what I'm talking about, and for those who don't, here's a brief history.

Once upon a time, there were things called audio cassette tapes. You could record music or whatever else you choose as long as you purchased the writable ones. You could also purchase them with the hottest new singles of the time, and they were referred to as Candles, which was short for Cassette-Singles. I remember buying some of our favorites together like Bobby Brown's "Don't Be Cruel" or "My Prerogative" and Janet's "Miss You Much," which Edzo gave me a hard time about buying but would listen whenever I played it. Then there was Paula Abdul's "Straight-Up", and who could forget Boston faves Bell Biv DeVoe's "Poison" or Whitney Houston's "I'm Your Baby Tonight." Man oh man, we had some good times together. It's hard to believe that

Edzo's gone. Even though we had grown apart after I left for college, I would always make an effort to catch up with him when I came into town. I remember his son was tragically murdered in Brockton around the same time my dad passed. I also remember how devastated he was and how I hated myself for not being there at the funeral. Of course, being the friend that he was, Edzo pretended it was okay, but I know he felt some kind of way, because I did and still do. I never got a chance to apologize for not being there for him like he often showed up for me as my protector.

I remember when I came out on Facebook, and some loser came for me on my page. Edzo was one of the first people to defend me and tell me how much he loved me and where the hater should go! I don't think I ever got to tell him how much that meant to me and how much I loved and appreciated his friendship over the years. Now, like so many others, he's gone, and because of flight restrictions and state lockdowns due to this virus, I never got the chance to see his face, hold his hand, pay my respects, or be in his presence one last time. So, instead, I wrote a letter. I know this may seem like a strange thing for some, but I've used this method several times in my life to move past traumatic experiences, and believe me when I tell you it works. Writing a letter to someone who has passed on is therapeutic and can provide important steps to your healing, especially if there is unfinished business or unspoken words you are holding on to. There's no right or wrong way to do it. Just be honest and authentic about what you are feeling and connect to it.

Before sitting down to write this letter, here are some of the things I did to prepare myself and create the space to make it happen. I'll share all of them with you now. Just remember that there is no right or wrong way to do this. What I'm sharing is only my experience in making it happen.

Step One:
Create or find a quiet, safe place to sit and think. Once you've done that, grab what medium makes you most comfortable when writing. It can be a journal, notebook, notepad, computer, phone, sketchbook, or whatever. For those who are more comfortable talking, a voice memo or recorder is also suggested.

Step Two:
Get anything out of your space that should not be there. By this, I mean any judgement or belief that you can't be real in this space that belongs to you.

Step Three:
Tell the person exactly what you're thinking or feeling, and remember this is only between the two of you unless you decide to share it with others. That means taking on anger, shame, hurt, disappointment, secrets, or whatever else connects you to them. Warning for some: this may be a little uncomfortable, especially if there are serious

unresolved issues. The good news is, this is your chance to get it all out. No matter how big or small, just let it produce itself.

Step Four:
Embrace every emotion and question that is present for you at this time. Examples: Why'd you leave me? Why didn't you fight harder? Were you in pain? Did you know how much I loved you? Did you know I was angry with you? Address whatever and however you're feeling.

Step Five:
Take in everything, as this will be one of the several steps in helping you find acceptance and begin the tough process of moving past this moment and into your healing.

Step Six:
Compose your thoughts. First, remember steps two and three. This can be anything from capturing special times shared, moments of appreciation, or disappointments. Something they've contributed to your life they weren't aware of, favorite memories, or things you'll miss. It can be regrets you have, something significant, or revelations you've had since their passing.

Step Seven:
The final step is deciding what you're going to do with

the letter once it's completed. This can actually be one of the hardest and most personal steps in this process. Again, it's important to remember there is no right or wrong decision when completing this last task. You may decide to:

- Keep it close to you, maybe in a book, a Bible, your wallet, or some safe place in your home.
- Send it to a friend or loved one who might appreciate it.
- Share it anonymously in a public forum, like a meeting, church, or even a memorial service for the deceased.
- Seal it up and keep it hidden away until you are ready to share it.
- Destroy it and never think about it again.

Or, like in my case and others featured in this book, you can share in a place where it will serve as a tool to help ease others' pain as they continue to find ways to grieve.

With that being said, I have included a letter to my best friend, Edzo, using the same instructions I shared with you to use when writing your letters.

Dear Edzo,

I hope you're somewhere in paradise reunited with your son. I'm sorry I never got a chance to meet him. I'm sorry I didn't attend his services when he was taken from you. I also hope you know just how much I absolutely loved and appreciated you and your friendship. I only wish I showed up as often as you did for me. It's not often that you meet someone who really loves you unconditionally from a space that is so pure, which can only be described as agape love. Sorry that, at times, I took that love for granted and allowed distance and years to separate us from being who we were in high school for so long. But you found your way back into my life on social media, popping up unannounced, coming to my rescue and defending me on Facebook like we'd never been apart. Till this day, I can't think of you without it bringing a smile to my face, especially when I remember our times together in class joking and capping on each other with Damon and Chris or our extended lunchbreaks. You were one of my first friends that I got a chance to know outside of the four walls of school, and you quickly became someone that I loved and trusted. So much so that I rode on the back of your motorcycle several times!

That probably doesn't seem like a big deal, but it was. You didn't know this, but I was petrified of motorcycles because of my great cousin, Delta, who lost both his legs due to a very bad motorcycle accident. So, even though I thought motorcycles were the coolest thing ever, I was never gonna own or ride one until I met you.

You helped me tackle a fear that I never told anyone I had, and because of that, I was able to ride with and without you carefree years after. I'm sure you're also partly responsible for me being the daredevil I am today. So, THANK YOU, my friend, for always making me feel safe when I was in your presence. I knew when I was with you nothing was going to happen to me, and not because you said so, but you showed it time and time again. Especially when you thought I wasn't paying attention to you threatening folks not to touch me or even look at me the wrong way. All the while defending your reasons or right to hang with me (the lil' preppy nerd) when I'd come chill at your crib after school or when my mom and the entire family would pull up in the "Michael Jackson" luxury van to drop me off at your spot in the middle of the hood. I can still see the looks on your neighbors' faces when I got out and waved goodbye as my family drove off with you cheering in the background.

The first thing we'd do is go grab some Chinese food and a couple of Hawaiian Punch. Then it was back to your place for some tournament-style Nintendo for hours.

God, I miss those days as much as I miss you and the simplicity of our relationship. You never sized me up, never made me feel like I had to explain myself, and you never let me pay for everything. That was pretty major since I had been working since I was thirteen and normally "that guy" in the company of most. Not to mention everyone always assumed that the "Cosby Kid" had it all. Thanks for letting me know that our friendship wasn't about what I had in my wallet, but instead what we both had in our hearts for each other; "Nuttin But Love." You will always be one of my favorite defenders, best friends, and the best Big Brother I never had.

I love you, Edzo. Until we meet again, rest in paradise, King, and tell Edzo Jr. that his uncle is dying to finally meet him! (No pun intended.)

Your Boy for Life & Beyond,
Cer Collins (The Lost Cosby Kid)

This letter was easy to write because there is no bad history between us. There was, however, a strong sense of guilt that was relieved by the fact that I know he never held it against me.

My next letter would be something completely different, as there is a bit of family drama and unresolved issues that made it hard for me to formulate my thoughts without trying to give meaning to things or take on things that were none of my business. As a child, my mother taught us to stay in a child's place, but even as a child, you tend to recognize when something is not right. My dad's sister seemed to fall into that category quite often. She was always involved with or in a situation that didn't match who I knew her to be.

My saved, whacky but highly intelligent, and fun Auntie Gwyn had a very distinctive voice that was only more pronounced when she sang. Her unique tone and vibrato were something I always enjoyed hearing, especially when she sang one of my favorites, "I Want Jesus to Walk Around My Bedside." Something about this song brought me both great joy and sorrow. I could only guess it's because I heard it mostly at funerals that it made me so sad. That song is one of the very first I can remember all of the Collins Family singing together. Even as I write this, I can hear my dad on the drums, Uncle Mike on the bass, my grandmother and Aunt Jackie holding the background and melody, and Aunt Gwyn leading the song. It brings a smile to my face and tears to my eyes. I can't believe there is no footage of the legendary Collins singers performing up and down the East Coast or in the many churches in Boston where they would always show up. Thank God for the good and bad memories--most fleeting, some complicated, and others jumbled.

Most of the time spent with Aunt Gwyn was in church or in the car as my dad drove her and my grandmother around to take care of church and other businesses. I remember her hugs, her smell, and her laugh no matter what was going on in her life. She and my dad always found a reason to laugh. When she and Uncle Mike divorced, I recall her being broken. She seemed lost, angry, and sad. Although I don't really remember what happened, that's also when her relationship with my mom also appeared to change. It still saddens me because I never knew what it was, and till this day, I still don't know. I only know my mom encouraged us to love them unconditionally, even though it was apparent something had changed. My mom didn't allow it to affect our relationships.

Over the years, as the family dynamic changed, both my dad's parents passed, and my aunt and cousins moved around. Our bonds stayed intact, and when I left Boston to go to the Savannah College of Art & Design where my cousin Mike attended school, Aunt Gwyn and I stayed in contact. She warned me to be careful while I was there but never gave me a real reason why, which always seemed weird. Maybe it was just a reference she made since my cousin dropped out of school for whatever reason; I'll probably never know. Our communication thereafter grew cryptic and soon nonexistent, but, no matter what, she was always Auntie Gwyn.

I remember after graduating and returning home to Boston, things seemed to be a little more strained between my mom and aunt. It was obvious that whatever it was had forever changed things. Yet, I still loved her and my cousins. Over the years, we've had our family issues like any other family, and like most, we worked through them without ever really discussing them. But when I got the call that she had passed, every avoided conversation, unspoken word, and missed opportunity for closure hit me like a ton of bricks. I was and still am devastated by the news. Mostly because I knew with the coronavirus being a very real threat, I wouldn't make it home to pay my respects, and even if I did, because of state lockdowns and social distancing restrictions, we wouldn't have a proper going home service. I was stuck with so many emotions and thoughts running through my head that I immediately grabbed my phone and began to write.

Dear Auntie,

I still can't believe you're gone, and even though I know you had been sick and in a lot of pain for some time, I never really tried on the fact that one day, like Daddy, you'd be gone. So many times, we prepared for the worst, and each time, you pulled through. So, it was a familiar dance we always knew the ending to. Never did that finale' include you being gone.

There is so much I want to know, so much I want to say to you, so many things I want to ask, but most of which I have no right to. So, I won't. I just want you to know that no matter what you may think of my mom, she respected you and the bond that you had with your brother, her husband, and my dad. She only wanted him to recognize that his family was now a priority in his life and that when he made those vows like her, his new family was now about her and his five kids. I sometimes feel like most of the struggle was to establish your place in my dad's life because of the challenges you had with the other men in your life. But rest assured you were and will forever be his sister whom he loved dearly and would protect with his life. There was never any room for competition because the love he shared for both you and my mom were undeniable. I'm sorry you were hurt, especially if any of that hurt came from me. Please know that you were my favorite aunt on my dad's side--the prettiest, the funniest, the most fun to be around, and the smartest.

If you ever thought I was told anything about you, that's untrue because I wasn't. Instead, I was asked to mind my business, be aware, and be respectful. I only hope that's what I gave you, even when it wasn't easy to do so. I enjoyed having you in my life, and I miss our phone conversations, your prayers, your encouragement, and most of all, your love and voice. I hope that in your final moments, you were not in pain and that you were at peace and that like that song you sang, Jesus was walking around your bedside waiting to take you home to be with the family once again and for eternity.

Daddy, Grandma, Poppa Deak, Uncle Sonnie, and Aunt Jackie, may you all rest in paradise. Until we can all be together again, keep Heaven lit.

Your First Nephew,
Cer XOXOXO

I've attached letters from family members in dedication of Gwyn, starting with my favorite cousin, Nichelle Mungo, Larechia Baldwin, and one from close family friend, Nahshon J.A. Deas to his dad.

Spencer M. Collins IV

To Mommy,

My dear sweet Mommy, I have many questions I am not ready to make public, and bear uncertainty if I ever will. You'd be so proud of us, though. The gifts of God, love, and togetherness you've imparted in us are integral to who we are today, and all is ever-present with us. So many compliments come to us and many have even expressed how our authentic closeness to each other is enviable. Many also comment on the love they feel when speaking to us, and every conversation about you is nothing but joy-filled.

We are finding so many nuggets of wisdom going through your things and feel you've prepared us all of our lives for this moment. We found your vinyls, too, and they still play! Your voice is so beautiful, Mommy, and filled with the precious Holy Ghost. All of us have your spirit within, and we are going to keep your beautiful legacies alive and well. Your prominence will continue to be known across this globe, Mommy, for you embodied love, inclusivity, community, and peace. I pray you knew how much you were loved and how many lives you impacted while here on Earth.

Though sicknesses plagued your body, you always had the strength to smile and praise God. You were our angel on Earth, and we all are receiving constant reminders and signs that you are very much so watching over us. There was a particular subject we didn't get to speak about in person, but we did many times in the spirit, and I am confident in God and through the special bond we had that you see me. I most certainly see you, and I'm in awe of your astounding greatness. You shared so much with me, Mommy. We were always bonding! Tears fall *as I write because I miss everything....our routine, our late conversations, your prayers (I have a few on video), your optimism in your own hurt for me in mine when carnality wanted to wrestle the flesh and blood we should not...*

These days without you are hard to take, and often I'm either repeating myself or sighing with an, "Oh, Mommy..." I just can't believe it most times, and when reality hits, I'm completely stifled. Though I know we shall all return to dust when God calls, it is hard to contend with the fact that the only guarantee in life is the most painful for those left to mourn. I love you so much, and I know you know this...and because of this, I honestly have peace amidst grief. I'm able to laugh and hold conversations of your greatness, and we have memories to last generations. You taught us well how to be moral and righteous.

The only thing I wonder is what life would have been had you physically come to live with us. We were ready for you, but God had other plans that even in hurt, we must relent to. I promise, my dear sweet Mommy, that I will celebrate your life every chance I get. Everyone will forever know Reverend Dr. Gwendolyn Collins-Stephens.

Love,
Nikki

Spencer M. Collins IV

Dear Aunty Gwen,

So glad I got the chance to talk with you the day before you went home. At the time, I didn't quite understand what you meant when you said you were "ready to go home," but after telling my mom, she explained it all to me. And even though I know you were in a lot of pain, I'm still over here struggling. Just going through a lot of emotions, asking why. I know God is watching over me and now you, but I've been having these funny headaches since you passed, and I don't really know why. But I am.

I'm just thankful I got a chance to see and hang out with you the weekend of Valentine's Day. I remember it put a big smile on your face and mine. I told you a lot of what I was dealing with that day, and I still remember the advice you gave me. Just to let you know, it worked. So, thank you.

I also remember you asking me to watch Dr. Pimple Popper with you, and my stomach was like, "Uhh, Satan, you're a liar." I definitely won't forget that experience anytime soon as much as I'd like to. LOL! The time spent with you was priceless!

I'm going to miss the times we shared together. I could always talk to you about any and everything. Thanks for always being a shoulder to cry on and an ear to bend. Till this day, I can't watch Dr. Pimple Popper without thinking of you and crying.

Love You To Life,
Larechia Baldwin

Dear Dad,

The coolest guy I know. I think you were the coolest guy in the world to me because you gave me permission to be different. To be an individual. Relishing and thriving as a gem, being the one and only me. You made a lot of people feel that way. After you transitioned, that love pours onto and into me from all who love you. That sounds like the gift that keeps on giving to me.

It's been two years since we have seen each other, and so much has happened since then that I don't even know where to begin. I finally moved to Los Angeles. The industry is so fake and fickle, and finding friends has been interesting. But I'm not worried about it. Just know (if you don't know this already) I carry every bit of your energy with me every day. It keeps me when I'm in the face of dogma.

In a world where there are a plethora of reasons to give up on this black man and go with the status quo, deep in my heart I know to stay true to what I know to be right. What you taught me is threaded in my choices, my work, and in the giving of my benevolence to others.

We are in a global pandemic, which I never thought I would experience in my lifetime. Things are literally crazy right now with worldwide deaths close to a million. Job losses for anyone not considered an "essential" worker. It's every man for himself out here. Quarantined at home for months, my guy! Crazy! But I've taken the time to work on content, getting caught up with loose ends, and taking the time to consider more of what really matters in life.

And although this experience has brought out the realness of who people really are, no matter what happens, I will never

Spencer M. Collins IV

not represent the values that you've instilled in me. With that, and the memories we have that no one can take away. And when I may be afraid at times, I am going to be ok.

"The work is never done when you lead with love."
"Te amo y te extraño mucho, este niño en crecimiento todavía necesita a su papá."

Hasta...
Shon

As you read the letters submitted in dedication to those lost, one of the things I hope you're getting is a sense of the relationship each person had with the deceased and how very different they are. This is a part of the process that will allow you to express your authentic feelings without feeling judged, and remember that your experience of something or someone belongs to you and you alone. No one can tell you how or what to feel nor can they express what only you can when describing what you had with someone else. Therefore, I strongly believe there is no right or wrong way to do this, only suggestions that will help you when trying to compose and express your thoughts. I'm excited for those of you who will choose to do this because I know personally the closure it can bring once you're finished. So, let's get to writing and actively chase our healing!

Chapter Five

April Fool's Day Stimulus Plan

Today is April 1st (April Fool's Day), and we've been talking about a relief package since mid-March, but once again, the current administration can't seem to come to an agreement. I even made a joke about it on my page and that of our local blogger, Tyeses Jackson. I don't think people found it funny, but he did. We laughed and talked about it, and he said, "The girls don't laugh when it comes to a coin." He was right because someone even messaged me instantly saying, "That shit wasn't funny." Okay, I get y'all ain't in a joking mood. Got it! But it is April Fool's Day and our fool (#45) was still trying to figure it all out.

At times like this, I miss President Obama. I know a lot of people didn't appreciate him, but most of them were people who don't really understand laws, legislation, and Congress. So, they didn't understand why he couldn't be this Great Black Hope everyone thought he would be when we elected him. I'm not one of those people obviously, because if it were up to me, I would have voted him in for a third term. Instead, I was with Miss President Hopeful, Hilary Clinton (who should actually be in office now), but we all know what happened. #45 cheated and the Americans let him get away with it, just like everything else he's done while he's been in office. That's the main difference between the Democrats and the Republicans. They are diehards for each other. We could learn a few things from them, but I digress. Now, where were we? Oh yeah, the stimulus and relief funds.

We are now three months into the pandemic. Cities and businesses are closed, and the economy is taking a beating. Unemployment is at an all-time low. Folks are unable to pay their bills and take care of their essential needs, and the government can't decide what to do about it. There's been several conversations, proposals, and debates, but still no definite answer to what needs to be done. Something needs to be done, but what could that be?

Back on March 13th, #45 declared a national emergency and suggested $50 billion to combat the effects of the coronavirus on our economy. On the 18th, he signed into law a relief package. This law also included free testing for COVID-19 and paid emergency leave, which was needed by millions of U.S. citizens struggling because of all the nationwide stay-at-home mandates. On March 27th, Trump finally signed the stimulus package into law, and we all sat back waiting for our checks. Now, I know I've mentioned this already a few times in the book, but what I haven't mentioned is that there are many, like myself, who are still waiting on the damn thing. Yep, I'm one of the millions that never received a check. Who knows where it is? An ex could have it. Maybe a crafty old neighbor has already deposited it into his or a friend's account, or maybe it's still sitting on #45's desk waiting for him to sign since he insisted they all have his signature on them. Child, personally, I don't care if he or Adolf Hitler signs my check. All I ask is you just PLEASE run me my coins. I don't know about y'all, but I could really use the extra thousand dollars. I know it's not much, but since most of us aren't working right now, that lil' something is better than nothing.

Now that I brought you up to speed, let's get back to what happened on April 2nd as 6.6 million workers filed for unemployment benefits. This is the highest number of initial claims in U.S. history. At the same time, we have reached a devastating milestone globally. According to John Hopkins tally, we have now surpassed one million cases of the coronavirus. As the virus continues to devastate the globe, we are still trying to figure out the best ways to protect ourselves. To wear a mask or not to wear a mask? Once again, there doesn't seem to be a clear answer as we watch press releases with some of the staff wearing them and others not adhering to it.

Just once it would be reassuring to see everyone on the same page, and perhaps, the hysteria that has been created would dissipate. Instead, we get more contradicting orders from the administration, like on April 3rd, when it was recommended that Americans must now wear "non-medical" cloth face coverings, which is the complete opposite of what was suggested previously when they said it was unnecessary for people who weren't sick. I strongly believe you understand the point I'm driving home. It's no wonder people aren't following the guidelines and regulations of this team that seems to be divided on every hand. While we try to figure it out, places like China, where the outbreak originated, are now reopening. With a total death toll of just over 46,000, they have managed to bend the curve and reopen Wuhan after a 76-day lockdown.

You would think the United States would use the blueprint of the other countries that's been laid out before us. Unfortunately, because of the arrogance of our leader who only chooses to conspire with others when it directly benefits his personal agenda, we haven't and probably won't, which is why our numbers will continue to rise. Thousands of vulnerable and innocent Americans will continue to lose their lives as a result. I hope and pray that I won't be one of them.

On April 14th, #45 halted funding to the WHO while a review was conducted. Some may ask, who is this WHO I keep mentioning. For those of you who don't know, WHO is the acronym for the World Health Organization. They are an agency of the United Nations and responsible for public health. The governing structure and principal's main objectives as "the attainment by all people of the highest possible level of health," their job is to keep the world safe by promoting health and serving the vulnerable. Ensuring that people have universal health coverage and are protected with better health and well-being.

A review is being conducted to determine the WHO's role in the mismanaging and cover-up of the spread of the coronavirus. This comes during the world's worst pandemic after it was accused of the same, in addition to having knowledge of the outbreak months before it hit America. Nothing surprises me when it comes to this president, his administration, or this country. However, it does give me a reason to reconsider some of the conspiracies I used to be so quick to dismiss as crazy. One of the latest being why Kobe Bryant's plane really went down, but once again, that's a whole different conversation and book, and I'm not trying to write that one.

Around the world, health officials, doctors, and task forces are trying to find ways to separate the infected from those who are negative or have already recovered from the virus. This will keep it from spreading to communities, especially in areas that are at a higher risk of developing the deadly virus. On April 20th, Chilean health officials announced that they will begin using the world's first digital immunity cards given to people who have already recovered from the virus. These cards will help identify individuals who no longer pose a threat to the general public. As I hear these new ideas, I can't help but wonder why the U.S. hasn't adopted some of these preventative measures. It's almost like they want us to get sick, like this is some kind of plan or "conspiracy theory" (ha-ha). You can imagine that. "A country that is evil enough to do such a thing by putting lives at risk for their own personal gain. Who could ever imagine a country like that?" he says sarcastically.

With suspicions that the coronavirus may have been in the U.S. longer than initially believed, states are beginning to wonder if certain reported deaths may have been mispronounced. But, on April 21st, in California's Santa Clara County, two autopsy reports showed that two deaths that occurred in mid-February actually passed from the novel coronavirus three weeks before the first known case was recorded in the United States. As that news unfolds, a week later, the U.S. surpassed one million known cases of the virus. Shit is getting real!

I don't have to tell those of you reading this what it's been like during this event of unfortunate circumstances, because we've all experienced some of the same things. Some of us have shared them, some of us never will. Some of us have posted about it, others never will. Some of us have even suffered in silence, not wanting anyone to know the devastating effect this has had on us.

On the flip side of things, I've also experienced

through social media the positive effects it has had on families. But I've never seen so many of us post about our siblings, aunts, uncles, nieces, and nephews. Quite frankly, I didn't even know some of you had families. My favorites have been the Mom & Dad videos, making me miss mine even more than I already do. I know my dad would have been more than willing to participate in some of the silly shenanigans I've seen. It also made me have a deeper appreciation for my mother, who is still here and part of the population that is at high risk because of her age.

Speaking of which, my mother had a birthday on April 30th, which makes her a stubborn, practical, and fiercely loving Taurus. This was also a milestone birthday. At this point in time, every birthday is a milestone considering the state of the world today. After watching countless Tik Tok and YouTube videos, Facebook, and Instagram posts, I wanted to do something special that would allow everyone to be a part of my mother's birthday without putting her life or anyone else's in danger. This meant not hopping a last-minute flight to Boston to surprise her like I normally do or sending her a ticket to come here to California like we've also done in the past. What could we possibly do to celebrate my mom and remind her just how special she is, not only to us but to our family and friends, as well?

After speaking with my partner and siblings, we came up with the idea of doing a virtual Zoom birthday party, but the problem was that most of us had no idea how to use Zoom. With the help of some incredibly special friends, whose names I will mention, not only were we able to pull it off, but it was something she'll never forget in her lifetime.

What made it special was that everyone involved who live here in Los Angeles are people she has met and has a special relationship with, such as my sister, Jessica Simington, my brothers, Apollo, Levine, and Rayshawn Grooms, Parnell Maracono, and William Scales, one of my oldest and dearest friends, Maya Williams and her son Rah-Jah, my roommate and family friend, Demar Singleton, known as DeJae, the fabulous Shaunte' Tabb-Massard, the beautiful Trisha Mann-Grant, my good friend American Idol Jacob Lusk, the talented Durand Bernarr, Elijah Jamal, and vocal beast (one of my mom's faves), my girl and big sis, Lettrice Lawrence.

I'm sure someone is wondering why I mentioned all their names. Because I think it's important to take time out to acknowledge those who take the time to always acknowledge you. Each person who took the time to send a message did that for Momma and me when they sent their videos. So, thank you, Family. We love you.

This next group of folks are the East Coast Family, and they did the same, starting with my godsister and my mom's miracle godchild, Michell Barzey, my cousins, Nichelle Mungo and Gwendolyn Jones-Dunton, longtime family friends, Cynthia Jones and Nahshon J.A. Deas, my beautiful and talented nieces, Dezvray Beasley,

Hannah and Deleyah Collins, my auntie and second momma, Marcia Moore, and of course my one and only child, Nico Ameire Titsworth-Priest-Collins. (Yep, all of those are his names).

Last but certainly not least, my siblings Delta, Rovenia, Cherayna, and baby sister, Kyriele, who I couldn't have done this without (not true and TRUE), and to my amazingly supportive partner, K, who's involved with everything I do and is my mother's favorite son-in-law. I can't imagine doing anything that I do without you. Every gay man has a wife that their mom, family, and friends approve of or wish for, and Ophelia Jessica Harper is this person. Thanks for always being a "YES" and for loving me unconditionally. You are definitely my wifey until some lucky man steals you away. I'm forever grateful to have you in my life, Queen.

Well, as you can see, April was a very busy month, and although we were knee-deep in this pandemic that doesn't seem to have an end in sight, it is very important that we live our lives as safely and abundantly as we can. Remember, this too shall pass (I don't know when) because nothing good or bad lasts forever. Remember to celebrate your friends, family, loved ones, and most importantly, yourself. During these dark times, it's easy to get caught up in the despair of it all. I know this to be true because for a while, I did. Thank God for surrounding me with people who wouldn't allow me to stay there, people who constantly reminded me that I'm not alone and encouraged me to ask for help when I needed it. Right now, we could all use a little help. Don't be afraid to ask.

Now that the party is over, let's get back to business. The stimulus checks!

Apparently, the first round went out about two weeks after the packages were signed into law, but I still had not received mine yet. I guess the first round was electronically deposited into some Americans' accounts. (I'm not one of the some.) According to the IRS, the first round was successful, and the next round of some 2.2 trillion dollars would be deposited next. They even had a website where you could check your status. All you had to do was type "Where's my money" or "Get my payment" in your internet search engine. Stop laughing. I'm serious. If you don't believe me, put this book down and try it. You'll end up right at the IRS.gov website. Then you just follow the directions. Unfortunately, every time I type in my info, I get this message: *PAYMENT STATUS NOT AVAILABLE.* Da fuq! You lying. Am I the only one getting this bullshit? You don't have to answer. I already know I'm not! #45 messes up everything, and this ain't no different. Seems like this is gonna be a problem, too. So, if you haven't filed taxes in a while, just forget about it, and if you have filed taxes but you still owe, then you can definitely forget about it. You know Miss FICA and greedy Uncle Sam (the relative nobody wants) always finds a way to get their money.

If you moved and didn't update your forwarding address, forget about receiving anything, and if you are a baby daddy that hasn't paid your child support, you can most certainly forget about it. Supposedly, if you're on SSDI or getting any other assistance from the state, they have your information, and if you didn't make the first round, you'll make the next. Well, at least that's what they say. Let me know how that works out for you? As for me, I pretended like it was never mentioned so that I could stop going to the site to put in my information every other day, hoping the message would change one day and give me a delivery date. I'm over it!

I have more pressing matters to tend to like finding out the results of this second COVID test and making sure I have enough food in the fridge to get me to next month, which by the way is my milestone birthday. I had a huge celebration planned to involve a mansion, caterer, deejay, performers, and all my family and closest friends. But given the circumstances, I don't think that will happen. Not only do I have to come up with other plans, but I have to fight with one of Airbnb's landlords, who refused to issue me a refund, and Hopper, who hasn't responded to my emails requesting canceling all these dag-gone tickets I can't use anymore.

I'm sure I'm not the only one fighting with these companies to get my money back, but I'm probably one of few who will openly talk about it, especially the long process of making it happen. I started my process back in March when we were issued the stay-at-home order. I thought for sure it was reason enough to request a refund, especially since I was canceling so far in advance.

Spencer M. Collins IV

I even disclosed my status and went on to explain that the people traveling to me were at high risk because of their ages, and still, I was denied a refund. After explaining myself several times to the owner, it was time to reach out to Airbnb's customer service and a supervisor for further assistance.

This is gonna get a little lengthy. So, I'll see you in the next chapter to talk about it. TTFN! That's ta-ta for now. I gotta go take my meds. This book is eating up my nerves!

Chapter Six

May-Day! May-Day!
We Have a Problem

Okay, in the previous chapter, I mentioned I was getting ready for my upcoming big birthday. Unfortunately, that meant coming up with alternative plans because of traveling restrictions and this whole COVID thing that doesn't seem to be going away anytime soon. I know #45 have some of you believing the summer heat will kill the virus, but that's a big lie. For months, he has suggested that as warmer weather comes to the U.S., the deadly "Kung-Flu" might "disappear" "like a miracle." These are his words, not mine. He continued: "Now the virus that we're talking about having to do -- you know, a lot of people think that goes away in April." He further buttressed his point saying, "Typically, that will go away in April." What he referred to as "that" in the statement is the coronavirus.

I don't know about you, but I try my best not to believe 85-90% of anything he says anymore. I used to give him the benefit of the doubt, but this dude is a pathological liar. He also went on to say, "There's been a rumor that you know -- a very nice rumor, that if you go outside in the sun or you have heat, and it does have an effect on the other viruses, but now we get in from one of the laboratories of the world." Again, I know you probably don't believe me, but these are all his quotes, and most of them make absolutely no sense. This is also the man that suggested on April 24th that we use ultraviolet light inside the body to kill the virus or inject disinfectant into the lungs or bloodstream. If this wasn't so incredibly stupid, it would be funny, but we have a man running the White House who thinks these foolish thoughts is embarrassing enough, yet he speaks them out loud. Every time I think he couldn't possibly get worse, he opens his mouth and proves me wrong. Anyway, with all that is going on in the world, you'd think it would be easy to cancel your vacation reservation and get your refund, but as I started to explain in the previous chapter, it has been a great challenge.

Since my birthday was coming up, I reserved a home in the hills of Malibu. I started communicating with the host in November of 2019 because I wanted to give myself enough time to plan and save accordingly. When we first started messaging, the response time was immediate. I sent a question and got an answer within minutes, and as my guest list grew, so did the questions and the host's answers. We laughed, talked, and joked about family, aging, weather, and living in California. We worked out a payment plan through customer service, and with everything set in stone, my birthday party was about to be lit!

I had already secured the deejay, the caterers, confirmed my guests, and was making the final plans when COVID hit. At first, we were all just watching, trying to figure out the direction of this virus, not knowing we would end up in a state of emergency since we were unable to travel, congregate in large groups, and restricted from having social events larger than a group of ten persons. I remember telling my family that I was thinking about canceling the event. Although they were looking forward to the festivities, no one wanted to risk traveling and being infected, and even if they wanted to, many airports were closed and flights grounded. There is a global pandemic, and many states are completely shut down, including California. So, when I contacted the host on March 15th and didn't get a reply, I was actually worried. First, I worried that maybe they were sick or someone in the family was infected, but as I continued to reach out with no response at all, I knew something wasn't right. It felt like they didn't want to respond immediately, but I wanted to give them time. So, I waited twenty-four hours before contacting them again.

I'd tell you this story, but I actually want you to see it with your own eyes. Because seeing is believing, and you have to see this to even begin to understand my frustrations.

March 15th (Me)

Due to the coronavirus and travel restrictions, a few of my guests are no longer able to attend. One has been quarantined, and it looks like I may have to cancel my plans to celebrate my birthday. I'm holding with Customer Care right now to go over the Extenuating Circumstances Policy now. I will definitely keep you posted!

March 16th (Me)

Follow-up text: Since I have a compromised immune system and won't be traveling anytime soon! Definitely not within the next few months, not until this pandemic is under control and there is some kind of treatment for this virus. Sorry for the inconvenience, but I need to cancel my reservations.

March 17th (Me)

Because of the current state of our country and my compromised immune system, I've been advised by my physician not to travel. Several of my guests have been advised the same and/or are unable or unwilling to travel any time soon because of the risk of being infected. Again, I apologize for any inconvenience this may cause, but I'd like to cancel my reservations at this time. Thanks in advance for your cooperation regarding this matter.

For those who know me and are reading this, I'm sure

you know that by now, I'm getting pissed because I can't stand being ignored. One of my biggest pet peeves is people not responding to my text and voicemail messages. It absolutely drives me insane, especially when I'm doing everything possible to keep it cute and professional. Not to mention that prior to my request to cancel, communication had been prompt and frequent. (Now that a brother is inquiring about canceling his reservations, you've gone mute.) These are the things that make black men like me look crazy, because like most African American males, I have a quiet storm brewing inside of me, waiting to erupt because someone tries to take advantage of me or treat me like less of a human being because of the color of my skin. This happens too often in America because whites know they can always get away with it, because the moment we show any emotion other than being happy, they feel threatened and will immediately pull the "Angry Black Nigger" race card. If I were a white man, I'd be irate, upset, or challenged, but as a black man, when I'm ANGRY or MAD, they're suddenly the victim. Keeping all that in mind, I decided to wait a couple of days to calm down and reach out one last time before I completely lose it and give them a token of what they're pushing me to be. Here's my next set of messages:

March 23rd (Me)
I'm reaching out again to request a refund as my family and I will be unable to travel due to the coronavirus and the effects

it's already had on my family. As I've already explained, I have a compromised immune system, and my parents and aunts are over the age of 60, which makes them most susceptible to the virus. Therefore, we will not be traveling anytime soon. Even when the mandates are lifted, we've been advised to travel with caution. I would think that given the severity of the situation you'd be more empathetic to what is affecting us all. I'm giving you plenty of notice to get the place rebooked if you believe that this virus isn't an obvious urgent threat. I'm making EVERY effort to resolve this issue without having it escalated. I'd appreciate at the very least some type of response! I look forward to hearing from you and resolving this issue soon.

Now see, that was very calm, very respectful, and straight to the point. Shit, I didn't even curse, but I can tell you right now with everything else going on in the world (and you know what I'm talking about), that this white host was about to make me lose it. Why in the hell aren't you responding? What's really going? Are they infected, and if so, why don't they have an automated response to let us know so I could be empathetic instead of staying uninformed and pissed off? Am I being a jerk right now or do I have every right to be feeling the way I was feeling based on the experience I was having? Sometimes as a black, I don't know because so often we can't show emotion for fear that it'll get us killed.

We can't cry; that makes us soft. We can't get angry; that makes us threatening. We can't be too loving; that makes us a bitch. So, who are we allowed to be?

Especially in this moment, when the color of my skin was the reason I was not being valued as a client or customer. I heard someone asking, "What does this have to do with COVID?" My answer is everything.

You see, being black in this very white America affects every single thing that we do. I can't even express myself in an email without thinking carefully about what I say for fear that it may cost me my life. That sounds ridiculous and dramatic. But let's say I went off the way I really wanted to, the way anyone that is being ignored would, and she decides to say she feels unsafe or threatened. All my information is in the Airbnb's database, and I know nothing will keep them from sending the police over to "give me a warning" or "arrest" me for harassment. Then, one wrong word or move, I would end up just like all the other unarmed, dead black men in America. These are the things white folks don't have to worry about or warn their sons about. Instead, all they're worried about right now is how to survive this new temporary crisis, while I worry about surviving being a black man in crisis-mode every single day. Everything reminds me that I'm not valued as a customer, a client, a patient, a man, or a human being.

Finally, she replied, and I could confirm that she was okay. I also know that she's been purposely ignoring me based on the correspondence we had prior, which was very different. No more playful conversation, small talk, or laughter because they got to show me who's boss.

March 23rd (Host)
Hi Spencer, I understand where you are coming from, but I'm unable to process a full refund for your stay. If you'd like to cancel now, I can offer you half of your stay as a refund as well as the cleaning fee. Other than that, I'm unable to offer more.

Say what? Oh hell no! I didn't get an apology for the delayed response. Not even a fake-ass show of concern, a "sorry to hear that", nothing. And do you know why? Yeah, I won't beat the dead horse. You get the picture, especially if you're an African American reading this, and also if you're a white person reading this and being honest with yourself because you know the first thing you would've gotten is an apology. Whether it is real or fake, it doesn't matter because it should be all about respect. What's sad is that we have grown so accustomed to this treatment that it has become a new normal, and we take that frustration back to our black-owned businesses and turn that displaced anger on them when they're in pain, too! However, that will be another book for another time. So, let's get back to business.

Before we go to my response, you should know that when I wasn't getting any response from the host, I called and further asked for a supervisor. I was told that it was under the discretion of the host to refund my money based on the extenuating circumstances. That propelled me to write an email to them, which follows. So, I already knew what could be done. Even though they responded, I practiced restraint and waited for them to prime wrong and do the right thing.

March 17ᵗʰ (Helpbot)

We know you've been waiting to hear from us, and we apologize for not responding sooner. Due to disruptions caused by the coronavirus (COVID-19), we're receiving a large number of requests right now.

If you would like to cancel your upcoming reservation, there's no need to contact customer support. Just request a cancellation from your Airbnb host. If your host agrees to the cancellation, no cancellation penalties will be applied to you or your host.

To request a cancellation, visit your Trips page and select the reservation you wish to cancel. From the drop-down menu, select the reason why you need to cancel. A request will be sent to your host, who will have 48 hours to respond.

If you would like to keep your reservation, you do not have to take any action. You can always visit our Resource Center for the most up-to-date information about how COVID-19 is impacting travel. www.airbnb.com/covid19

Now did y'all catch that? The first thing I got was an apology, so now I'm a little calmer. Next, I got the willingness to refund my money, especially given the circumstances of coronavirus. I absolutely hate making everything a Black & White issue, but if you've been living on this planet long enough, you tend to know how all things play out. However, I have to tell you that just like some white folks experienced the same thing at the same time, it is an everyday occurrence for us. That is the part of the conversation that always gets dismissed. Yeah, your life matters, too. But yours matters every day, and ours doesn't. So, the next time you hear someone chant **"Black Lives Matter"**, remember this and chant along, or do me a favor and **SHUT UP!**

Now back to the scheduled program, here is my response to the host, who still didn't know I had already spoken with a supervisor. Even after I let her know what I was told, she insisted on dragging this out, triggering my anxiety not to mention my natural desire and instinct to cuss her completely out. But, first, I needed to secure my $6,000, or there's 'bout to be some problems.

March 23rd (Me)

I don't understand why you can't offer a full refund when I was told it was under your discretion. Thanks for the response. I'd like to explore other options given the circumstances of what we're facing. This is not something I want to do. It's something I have to do, and with the Extenuating Circumstances Policy, I would think this would DEFINITELY qualify.

March 23rd (Host)

Hi Spencer, under the Extenuating Circumstances Policy, I do not think that this qualifies, but you're welcome to reach out to

Airbnb, as they may be able to provide additional guidance to us both. Thanks.

March 23rd (Me)
Thank you. That is a GREAT idea. I was actually advised by them to reach out directly to you so that we could work it out. But it seems like we both could use their assistance in this very unfortunate matter. I'm willing to negotiate something that makes sense to us both, but 50% is a no for me. Especially given the circumstances of EVERYTHING going on, including all our current financial statuses.

They are really trying it right now, and if we were living in person right now, I probably would have flipped a table by now or snatched somebody off the counter. But we're not, and I need my coins back unpenalized and untouched the full month. So, I'm going to do this back and forth thing for as long as I need to, even though customer service has agreed with me that the host is the one that has to approve the refund.

I know some of you are gagging in disbelief right now, and the rest of you have to go get a drink or smoke because this is bringing back memories of similar circumstances. Then there's still some of you who refuse to believe this is happening. I mean, how can she just not refund me my money? This went on from March until April, nearly a whole month of making excuses. I was even told this might prevent them from making their mortgage payment. Oh, boo hoo! I didn't believe them, and even if I did, that's their problem. They are the ones living up in the hills above their means, not me. I only wanted to rent it for the weekend.

It has been four days since we talked, and I was trying to figure out what was going on. By now, I've spoken with customer service again, and they are adamant that the host has to approve this transaction. So, I had to reach back out to the host.

March 27th (Me)

Good morning! Just giving you a quick update and making a suggestion. I've reached out to another customer service rep who suggested again that we do a mutual cancellation. I've done this in the past, allowing the owner to issue a full refund. Given the circumstances, I hope this is something you'd consider and maybe didn't know was an option, but it is. I know with no uncertainty that my family will now not be traveling for the rest of the year given what we are all experiencing. I only hope we can get this finalized and resolved as soon as possible so that it is no longer a part of this already horrific equation.

March 27th (Me)

Good morning. Last we communicated, you seem to be under the impression that your hands are tied in this matter. However, that is not the case. You used the words "unable to process a full refund," suggesting that if you could, you would. After speaking with several reps once again, I'm telling you that is an option. Under MUTUAL-CANCELLATION

POLICY, I can be issued a full refund at your request and approval. The only thing keeping this from happening at this point is you. I've been advised to resubmit my request and will do so today so that you can accept and approve it. Once done, this will conclude our business, and we can start adjusting to our new normal COVID lives. I look forward to your response.

March 28th (Me)

Please contact customer service so they can explain to you what they've already explained to me regarding the refund. Under the "Mutual-Cancellation" policy, a full refund can be issued. They asked me to resubmit, but the system won't allow me to without your approval. I keep getting this error message. (see attached)

March 28th (Host)

Hello Spencer, I just want to be clear there is no way that I can agree to a cancellation or refund on my side. This has been a really crazy time for everyone, and I totally understand where you are coming from. I've been personally affected by this as well and will likely lose my home. Airbnb's changes made to its policies several weeks ago devastated hosts like me. It's insane that even with existing cancellation policies, hosts had to take on all of the responsibility to refunding guests. Not sure what will happen to Airbnb after all of this is over. On top of that, guests should be focused on travel insurance and Airbnb, not hosts. If you can't get a refund from Airbnb through their policies, then there absolutely is no way I can go beyond them (they are already absurd), and respectfully, I ask you to be

87

reasonable and not continue to ask me to do something completely one-sided or unfair like that. If you really want to cancel, the best I can offer you is a 25% refund if you do it now.

March 28th (Me)

Are you serious? You went from offering half to 25%? This is COMPLETELY unacceptable, and I'm even more confused and frustrated by your response, especially because it seems like neither you nor Airbnb is trying to take responsibility for what is going on. Am I to understand that you are refusing to honor the "Mutual-Cancellation" Policy that several reps from Airbnb have suggested we do for me to be refunded? I need clarification before I take this to the next level. Implying or suggesting that your home is in jeopardy because of changes that have occurred with Airbnb suggests that someone is not being completely honest with me about what can and cannot be done! I'm being told each of you is responsible for honoring my request, but you both are saying it's out of your hands! At this point, maybe it is, so I'll seek outside advice to get this resolved, whatever that calls for.

I was officially over it and began communicating directly with customer service. I resolved within me that I will never use Airbnb again. I don't understand how the host has the power to refuse company policy and not issue the customer a full refund based on COVID-19 extenuating circumstances. Part of the relief package was to assist companies affected by the virus. I'd say this has a pretty big effect on both them and me; this whole experience has been draining, time-consuming, and traumatic. I should be compensated alone for emotional distress, and if I were a white woman, I'd consider a lawsuit. But as you can clearly see, they don't pay us any kind of attention.

March 29th (Me)

G'Afternoon, Ella! I've reached out to the host again with the information you gave me regarding the Mutual-Cancellation Policy. She still insists that there is nothing she can do and that her hands are tied because of changes Airbnb has made, tying the hands of the host. I don't know what this means, as I only have information that suggests what every rep I have spoken to has suggested in order for me to get a refund. I don't want this to be a never-ending request. How do we get this resolved once and for all? Even according to their own policy, I qualify for a refund, but she's talking in circles as you are, too! All I want is to be treated fairly. Provisions and bailouts have been approved to assist small businesses and corporations struggling through this pandemic. I'm sure you'll benefit from that as should I. My trip is being canceled out of necessity. My immune system is compromised, and I can't travel nor can several individuals in my party. This is a REAL issue and concern and should be handled by both parties as such. I do not understand why the host is not complying with your company policy. Perhaps you should reconsider your partnership.

March 29th (Airbnb Support)

Hi, apologies for the delay in response. Reservations for

Spencer M. Collins IV

stays and Airbnb Experiences made on or before March 14, 2020, with a check-in date between March 14, 2020, and April 14, 2020, are covered by the policy and may be canceled before check-in. If your check-in date is not covered, then the cancellation policy of your host will apply. We suggest that you contact us closer to your check-in date since the situation is rapidly developing.

March 29th (Me)

I'm patiently waiting it out. Just got news of another lost family member to this virus, so I think right now we are trying to figure out how to move forward so we can put this behind us and concentrate on what's really important. I'm very disappointed with this whole process and some of the responses I've spoken with thus far, but I will deal with it late. In the meantime, do what you have to do, and I'll do the same to make sure I get the refund that is owed to me by any means necessary. "Very Disappointed & Frustrated Customer"

April 10th (Airbnb Support)

I am so sorry to hear about that. The current COVID-19 Extenuating Circumstances Policy covers our hosts and guests with eligible reservations. Our policy takes into account official guidance from and restrictions by relevant governmental and health authorities and the World Health Organization.

We highly value the well-being of our traveling community, and after reviewing your request, we're able to confirm that your reservation does fall within our COVID-19 Extenuating

Circumstances Policy, which you can review here: airbnb.com/help/article/2701. To obtain a full refund, you will need to cancel your reservation. Please login to your Airbnb account and navigate to: Trips > Trips > Change or cancel > Cancel reservation > Select the reason: My travel plans have changed due to the COVID-19 pandemic" Complete the request, and don't hesitate to let us know if you have any questions or concerns.

Finally, it was over, and I would not have to communicate with them anymore, even though it would take an additional 14 days before I was officially issued a refund. Though this doesn't seem like a big deal to some, these are the kinds of things that can trigger someone in a fragile state of mind, who is already dealing with mental wellness issues, to take their own life or somebody else's. In this case, definitely somebody else's, several somebody else's, and YEAH, I know it sounds crazy, but when dealing with depression, everything seems more serious than it actually is. There were times things became so heavy while dealing with this and everything else I've shared that I actually contemplated the thought myself. It wasn't because of this one isolated incident but because of the many things that were happening simultaneously.

Not being able to work, not being able to make money or go out, constant trips to the ER, doctor appointments, no gym, no malls, no physical contact with the outside world would take its toll on a healthy human being. But one dealing in a history of depression, HIV, and Congestive Heart Failure, whose outlets have all been stripped away, this is truly a recipe for disaster.

With the help of my good friends, family, and loved ones, I was able to avoid those dark places as they were constantly checking in just to let me know someone cares and that my life matters.

A smile or a "hey" goes a long way when you're unable to get out. So, while we're all locked away trapped in our homes, pick up your cells, home phones, computers, and call somebody to say, "Hello. I love you," "Thinking about you," or simply ask how they are holding up. Then be prepared for whatever the answer is. The truth is, most of the time we just want to be heard. That's all. No unsolicited advice, no judgment. Just you focusing on listening and every once in a while, repeating what's being said back to them in the form of a confirming sentence or question.

- What I heard you say is...(paraphrase what they mentioned.)
- Sounds like what you're saying is...
- Summarize what was said.
- What did you mean by...?
- Did I hear you correctly when you said...?

All these are clear signs that someone is actively listening. I think they could've used this skill at Airbnb, because I certainly didn't feel valued or heard at all. Most people think our biggest problem is being pulled over and shot down in the streets by police, but what we deal with as Black people is a lot more complex than that. Our struggles extend the reaches of the street and into our schools, homes, workplaces, and affect every aspect of our lives through systemic racism and the residual effects of Jim Crow Laws. We can't undo what's been done over the course of four hundred years overnight, but we can reverse the effects one day at a time starting with reparations. An acknowledgement that what our ancestors endured at the hands of white Americans was not only inhumane and horrific, but the reason why our race remains far behind others when it comes to economics, generational wealth, and racial equality. Until this happens, these conversations will continue to confuse, upset, or make folks uncomfortable because they refuse to see the need or understand how it relates to so many different topics, including this one. Yes, the way I was treated by Airbnb has everything to do with the fact that I am a black man, and if you can't see that, I challenge you to figure it out.

Now let's continue to talk about other significant events that happened in May, leading up to my birthday. Now that I've given you a recap of March and April, it's important to know that while the virus was spreading, people were losing their jobs, homes, and some of their hair because of all the stress that was going on. That's not to dismiss what was happening, only to acknowledge the choice to live, and it's one we all have to make to get through this, especially as things were rapidly changing.

It was the first day of May, and I heard on the news that FDA Commissioner, Stephen Hahn, said that Remdesivir is the first authorized drug to treat Covid-19. If I'm not wrong, this is also the same drug they used to treat Ebola patients. So, does that mean the virus is a distant cousin of Ebola? If so, why haven't they announced that or at the very least given the information during a press release? Oh yeah, because they still have no idea. So, how can they treat you for something they don't have any research or clinical evidence about. Again, this is why I don't trust these doctors and so-called experts, simply because they operate under a blanket of lies and secrets. All I wanted to do was make it to another birthday. Can somebody PLEASE tell me how to do that, please? I'm on day two of my thirty-day countdown that started yesterday, and I've been trying to figure out just exactly what I'm going to be allowed to do in the new "Rona World" that we're living in. I can't travel for sure, and others can't travel to visit me, but can I at least finally have some company without being afraid we're going to infect each other? What's the latest reports? Do we have any good news? As the day ends, and I prepare for day three of my thirty-day countdown, I was suddenly hit with another panic attack. I was not sure what triggered it this time or if it was even a panic attack, but all I knew was that I was ready for this all to end.

I was trying desperately to get out of this funk

because I didn't want to be depressed, alone, and quarantined for my birthday. We've been locked down for months, and social distancing fatigue was starting to take its toll on me, which is why there's so many of us experiencing such a wide range of emotions. Folks are more angry, aggressive, irritated, agitated, and violent than ever before. You'd think something as horrific as this would bring us closer together, but it did not. I talked to friend and therapist, Anthony Margain, who suggested I start meditating, listening to less television and take on new exercises like guided imagery, daily walks, or bike rides while following social-distancing guidelines. Of course, anything else instead of continuing to stress myself out with daily press conferences that do nothing but give us more bad news about the virus. At his suggestion, I stopped but not before hearing that the president's administration had given eleven billion dollars to states to expand COVID-19 testing. This actually helped to keep my mind at ease until I heard Dr. Mike Ryan suggest that coronavirus may never go away and would join a mix of other viruses that kill people around the world every year.

This was not exactly what I wanted to hear as I was still trying to figure out what I would do for my 50th birthday, and folks were calling to ask if I'd still consider traveling to Cancun for our 5th Annual LGBT Music Festival. My answer? Hell no, are you crazy? Are you not paying attention to the news? But then I realized that most people don't have compromised immune systems, so they don't have to worry about the same things I do. This is not normal behavior for folks to be constantly worried about being exposed to a virus opportunistic infection that could suddenly end their lives. That was my sword to bear, and I needed to do it alone, which meant looking out for myself and doing what needed to be done to keep myself safe. Guess that means no party, unless I do a virtual party like the one we threw for my mom during her birthday.

It sucks that these are the thoughts and the types of conversations we engage in when it comes to events, parties, and social gatherings. But this is our new normal for the rest of the year and maybe beyond. In the meantime, the numbers just keep growing, and just three days before my birthday, John Hopkins University reported that the coronavirus has killed more than 100,000 people across the U.S. That's an average of almost 900 people a day since the first known coronavirus-related death was reported months ago.

I'm still not sure how we got to this number when we've seen what it's done to other countries. What did we not do to keep this from happening? Aren't people adhering to the mandated lockdowns? Aren't people staying in their homes, observing social distancing, and wearing masks? Oh yeah, NO, because at the beginning of this outbreak, our president led us to believe there was no imminent danger for us and that this was all a hoax. That's why we're dying now and the reason so many more will die before we get this threat under control.

This is another reason why when election time comes up, we need to get out and vote this monster out of office, because another four years under his administration may wipe us all out. A reality TV president! What the hell were we thinking? We might as well have elected a wrestler, basketball player, or rapper into office. I'm pretty sure they wouldn't have done any more damage than him.

Imagine Dwayne Wade as president and First Lady Gabrielle Union. They'd surely post a message of love for the LGBTQI community, and maybe folks wouldn't have been on his head the way they were. Their daughter Zaya could've been the head of the LGBTQI Taskforce, promoting transgender rights with Jayceon Terrell Taylor (*The Game*) as her first aid and protector. The inauguration would've had half of the NBA in the audience and former President Obama and my favorite First Lady, Michelle, as honored guests. Or President Dwayne Douglas Johnson and Vice President Kevin Hart, because you know those two are inseparable these days. First Ladies Lauren Hashian and Eniko Parrish would add all kinds of adversity in the White House. Imagine that inauguration. It would look like a movie premiere, and the White House would never be the same! With the Rock's giving spirit and Kev's sense of humor and compassion, this nation would be all smiles, and no one would be homeless or under the socio-political culture.

I'm just saying. I don't know about y'all, but I'm here

for it all. If we're going to just put anyone in office, let it be productive, loving, caring, and compassionate people who represent the best of who we are, instead of some loud-mouth narcissist dictator who can't even manage his businesses. But I digress, and unfortunately, that is not our reality. However, it could be!

I remember we all thought there was no way #45 would be elected. Yet, here we are at the end of his four treacherous years in office. I know they do divorce parties, but do they do "Thank God He's Outta Office" parties, too? Because if so, I'd love to host one, virtually of course. I imagine that some of you may think I hate him, but I don't. I just hate what he has reduced this country to. Not that it was ever perfect, because it wasn't. But that's part of what made his M.A.G.A. campaign so ridiculous. America "the land of the free" has always been about taking over marginalized communities and cultures so that they can remain the dominant species. However, it used to mean something to be an American. Now we're laughed at and a universal joke. We've lost allies, respect, and our dollar loses its value more and more every day. I wouldn't be surprised if they start banning us from other countries, thanks to this fool.

I know that was a lot, but that's what goes on in this head, especially with all that we are dealing with on a regular basis. I need to entertain something besides the Rona Shit, or I'm going to end up in a psych ward somewhere. After talking with the village and my family, I'm super excited about the karaoke-themed virtual birthday party. I was so excited that I decided to have my first guest over since February! I had my Lysol on deck, extra masks, gloves, and towels just in case folks needed to take a shower. I'm just saying. My folks would do anything to protect me, that's all.

I can't believe I'm half a century years old. I never thought I'd make it this far being a Black man with HIV and CHF, not to mention all the other shit I'm dealing with. Yeah, I know I mention it a lot, but when I think of all my healthy friends who are no longer here, and those that passed with HIV/AIDS, heart conditions, cancer, or whose lives were taken violently or unexpectedly, I realize that I don't have to be here. I probably shouldn't be, but I am, and it's the reason I use my voice the way I do. I have so much to say, so much to tell, and most of it would blow your minds. People think they know my story, but they don't, and they're not ready to know. All I know is that GOD, Mother Universe, Buddha, Jehovah, Allah, or whatever you may call he/she is REAL, and I know that for certain because I'm still here. By GRACE, I'm still here!

On May 30th, 2020, I remember being woken up with a soft kiss, a strong hug, and a HAPPY BIRTHDAY followed by a series of soft and masculine strokes that led to a 30-minute session of pure ecstasy. There's nothing like starting off the day with a good release, especially a birthday release to remind you that you're still here and everything still works.

As I got myself together and checked my texts, post,

and voicemail for well wishes and b-day love, I heard his phone ring, and the next time he appeared, he was fully dressed, rushing me to get up for a ride. Mind you, I was still in the awe of the after-sex glow, and he was about to take me out of that moment by rushing me up. But you know what? Even though I was cursing in my head, I wanted to honor this man and allow him to celebrate me in any way he wants. So, I got up and took my time to find something good to wear. I haven't been out in a minute, and it's my birthday. So, I gotta dress it up a lil'. Y'all know what I mean. Even though I had no clue where we were going, it didn't matter because he was looking DELICIOUS as usual, so I needed to look tasty, too, and wash out this mouth. He usually leaves the house before me, which normally makes me feel rushed, but not today, because I would have to take my time. You know why? Because it's my birthday.

After about fifteen or maybe twenty minutes. I was ready to feel and look cute and was excited to get outta this damn house to do whatever this wonderful man has planned. As I got to the end of the walkway, I saw a cute and familiar-looking girl holding balloons, and out of my peripheral vision, a striking handsome chocolate figure lurking on the side. It wasn't until they yelled SURPRISE that I was able to focus long enough to see that these were my folks.

Yes, my Cali sis, Jessica, sexy comedian and friend, Fo-Life Sampson McCormick, and my lil' bro, Sidney Ginyard, all were there holding signs, drinks, balloons and cards to surprise me for my birthday. How can I not mention my other brother, the handsome, sometimes annoying, always entertaining, late but best believe present, Marwan Granville. No matter what, he always shows up late. Yeah, it is not the extravagant private celebration I planned, but it's the next best thing considering the circumstances. I'm beyond blessed to have K as a partner and friend, and my village is part of the reason I'm still here. I know we all have folks who we call friends, and there are levels to those relationships that only you and them can understand. So, whenever you hear me refer to someone as the village, know that they are more than just friends; they are family. These are the people that know and love all of me unconditionally. The ones that know my mood swings, my smart-ass mouth, my highs, my lows, my faults, and my strengths, and they remind me to take my meds. With them, my mask is always off. I don't have to wear my super-ability cape or pretend not to be in pain or anything else other than what I'm actually feeling. Everybody should be lucky to have a group of friends like this. I know I am, which is why their names are mentioned throughout the book. If I didn't mention some names, know that they may not have been here physically but were all on the call along with 75+ other guests that showed up virtually to celebrate me. Needless to say, that I had a pretty epic 50th birthday celebration.

Remember all the masks, gloves, disinfectant sprays and everything else I mentioned earlier. Well, after the first thirty minutes together, we got so comfortable that we forgot about using them. I mention this because I know how judgmental I've been about people not wearing masks and adhering to all the rules. I mentioned it to serve as an apology to you, the reader. I understand how we can let our guard down; we get so caught up in the moment we forget that wearing these masks is for our own protection. We must be careful not to put us all at risk. (Sound familiar?) Not practicing safety is how HIV/AIDS spread so quickly through our community. So, do yourselves a favor and mask up. It may save the life of someone you love.

Dear Coronavirus,

The devastation you have caused since coming to America has been deadly, but we don't blame you for being what you were created to be. We blame those that may have manufactured and allowed you to invade our lives without warning. We blame those that have failed to take on the role of our leader and protector, not setting a plan in motion that would have curved or stopped the rate of infection and saved the lives of millions. Those that hid the existence of such a virus to protect a country's name. Those who hoarded supplies to be better prepared to respond when the virus outbreak spread.

Even though you've taken innocent lives and have single-handedly destroyed businesses and closed corporations, we know you are only being what you were created to be—a distraction, a scapegoat, and a reason to crash the market so that the already failing economy could be reset.

A bioengineered weapon created to rid the world of the weaker population, a genocidal masterplan. You were sent to create chaos, widespread panic, and strip us of hope, making us more dependent on the government. And while all that has happened, what has also happened is that we've turned more to our creators.

While conspiracy theories continue to grow, maybe you were sent here as a warning, maybe a punishment, or maybe just a way of bringing us back to our creator (who or whatever that is). No one knows the real answer, so maybe we should be thanking you for slowing us down and giving us more time with our families, more time with ourselves, an opportunity to create, rest, or to just be and breathe. Again, who really knows?

Spencer M. Collins IV

I certainly don't. So, wherever you came from, I just want to say that as of today, I'm taking back my life, my mind, my hope, and my belief that like I've survived other challenges, this too shall pass.

Child Of God & Believer,
Cer Collins

Chapter Seven
Reclaiming My Life

Now that I'm a year older and have made my peace with coronavirus, it's time I get back to work. I know I have to be careful, and I will, but I can't continue to be stuck in the house at the mercy of this virus. This is not the first pandemic, and it won't be the last. Though I'm petrified, I will no longer live in fear.

Today is June 2nd, and the party is officially over. Now it's time for the after-party called LIFE. Yeah, I'm still listening to daily reports of this Rona life, but they are landing differently now.

Wuhan has announced that they've completed a 9.9 million coronavirus test on its residents and have found no new cases. Things are already changing because that's what things do; nothing stays the same. Unfortunately, things have changed here, too, and we have passed the two million mark for confirmed cases here in the United

States. That means we've still got work to do. Although #45 keeps inheriting the blame for this rapid rate of infection, what have we done personally to contribute to decreasing the number and stopping the spread of this virus?

We know what his part was in all of this, but are we holding others accountable for their actions, as well? That includes you. Yeah, I'm talking to YOU. Are you washing your hands enough? When you come home, do you take off your clothes and bag them up or put them in the washroom to be cleaned? Do you hop in the bath or shower to wash off the germs? When you're outside, do you wear your mask? It's high time we took accountability for what we're not doing. I don't know all of what they're doing in other states, but I know enough to know they could and should be doing more.

Here in Los Angeles, Mayor Gavin Newsom laid out a plan since day one that would have certainly curved the spread of the virus if we had followed it, but folks weren't always doing what was requested or required. Folks were still partying, going to the beach, not wearing masks, opening businesses, looting, robbing, killing, and potentially exposing themselves and loved ones to the virus. Now listen, I know with the recent killings of George Floyd on May 25th (just five days before my birthday) and Ahmaud Arbery on June 24th--not to mention countless other unarmed black men and boys-- that we have a lot to be angry about. However, I'm not sure right now is the best time for these protests, but as I said that out loud and wrote it down, I realized no time has been the best time for protest. We have to do what we have to do when we have to do it, and with the increase of blatant attacks on African American males, the time is now. I just hope that while we're out there protesting BLM (Black Lives Matter), we're protecting them by "doing what needs to be done". I wish I was able to be a part of the movement, too, but with having asthma, CHF, and HIV, I think I should probably go sit down somewhere.

I've been contributing to the cause by making donations, making posts that keep others updated on what's happening, and discussing what this movement is really about with my non-black counterparts and how important it is to be a part of this movement. I get so angry when someone says to me, "All lives matter, not just black lives." When I hear such, I immediately want to jump down their throats, screaming defensively why the three words "Black Lives Matter" are so important. So, let's take the time to go there now, even though I believe at this point that most of the world understands after seeing multiple recordings of cops shooting unarmed black men without cause. I'm trying to be careful with my words because I hear people say, "He got shot for no reason." Truth is, there was definitely a reason, but the question is, was there cause? Most of the time the answer is no, which is why we must dismantle white supremacy and end the racial violence against black. They are not just targeting men; they are attacking our black women, too. Maybe not with the same viciousness but with the same intentions. This broken system needs to be fixed. It is not okay to shoot me or choke me out just because I'm black. Yet, that's what's been happening since Emmett Till. Quite frankly, if I have any non-black friends that need me to explain any further, we no longer need to refer to each other as friends. I'm so over the conversation when the evidence has been there in their faces for years. These killings and slayings of black men are not new; they're just more frequently recorded and posted, which makes it harder to ignore.

And while the two cases I mentioned are so widely publicized, my dear, beautiful sister Breonna Taylor, who was gunned down in her home back in March, still hasn't received justice. Louisville Metro police officers Jonathan Mattingly, Brett Hankinson, and Myles Cosgrove still haven't been charged for taking her life and stealing another light from this world. Say their names, not hers. Say their names because these officers rarely get mentioned in these senseless slayings. In fact, most of them get to go on with their lives like nothing happened, under the radar without us blasting them and letting it be known to the world who these murderers are. So, "Say Their Names."

On June 4th, I received a call from my good friend and mentor, Paul Scott. Gay Pride was coming up, and he was letting me know of a meeting that he felt, as an activist, I should've been invited to--The Black

Leaders/CSW Roundtable discussion on the upcoming festivities and what that should look like this year with the pandemic happening simultaneously with the current protest and BLM movement. Now, at first, I wasn't going to attend. I hate showing up where I'm not welcomed or invited, and though it's fun to crack a face or two with your presence, I was actually hurt that I wasn't asked to be a part of the discussion and wasn't feeling it. Paul reminded me that being a board member, I should definitely be in attendance. So, I swallowed my pride and bruised ego and inserted myself into the space as only a listener at first.

As the conversation reached an uncomfortable and climatic peak, I decided to chime in. It seemed like there was tea, and the kids didn't want to part with Christopher Street West because of its history of racist behavior towards the black community. The girls were all in an uproar, but most of what I heard were personal grievances that, like me, really had no place on the call. LOL! Yes, CSW was definitely guilty of the crimes but wanted to atone by inviting us to be a part of something that was bigger than anyone's hurt feelings, I thought. So, while others complained, argued, criticized, and judged, I simply pointed out the benefits of this momentous occasion and event happening. I'm sure my comments weren't really welcomed or received with any kind of respect, considering the call was full of folks I've had issues with in the past, but in that moment, it didn't matter. All that did matter was that we took advantage of this opportunity to partner with BLM, who didn't really have a space for the LGBTQI community prior to this meeting and the ginormous amount of press that would be there to capture this act of solidarity, giving a bigger voice to two disenfranchised communities. Sounds like a win-win to me, and so after expressing my opinion and reaching out to other organizers to offer support and gratitude, I then prepared myself for what was about to happen next.

First, I came home and told my Rock what I planned on doing to get his opinion on everything, including being in a large crowd of people and then coming home to him. He was confidently and completely comfortable with it, especially since he had been giving me vitamins, herbs, home remedies, and concoctions to rebuild and strengthen my immune system. However, when it came to the march itself, that was a different story.

You see, he feels like Blacks always diminish our fight by inviting others into it, whereas other nationalities fight for what they want without feeling the need to do the same, and with a clear agenda and call to action, which we lack.

Black lives have to matter to us first before we try to convince the world with a declaration that we don't even uphold. We are still killing each other in the streets, disrespecting our elders and ancestors with our toxic behaviors. We need to address these issues amongst ourselves before inviting others in. It's okay for them to support us, but we can't start including them by adding pronouns "ALL" to the already complete message. If you are Black and queer, straight, bi, or trans, because you're black, you are already included in the message. Adding anything to it is just not necessary in his humble opinion. I agree with him, especially when it comes to us looking for validation from others and including them. I'm not saying I don't want them there or their support, but what I'm saying is that we don't NEED them there.

He also went on to say that when the marching is all over and it's time to sit down and discuss the needs of our people, we need to include the elders that have already done the work and research to know exactly what it is we need. Elders like Dr. Claude Anderson, Minister Louis Farrakhan, Dr. Boise Watkins, and Dr. Frances Cress Welsing, who know what the code of conduct should be moving forward. Like demanding what's owed to us in the form of reparations for our Black Holocaust, and for the land, cities, homes, and banks that were stolen from us and passed down to generations of white folks that did nothing to earn it. All we ask for is what's fair, and that's giving back what was stolen from us. It's the only thing that will begin to get us back on track. Bae is a scholar when it comes to this subject, so I love conversing with him about it. However, I can't let his opinion, as valid as it is, keep me from being a part of this historical moment. No more than I can allow my fear of getting infected keep me trapped in the house and my mind. It's time to "Stand Up."

I'm here and standing on the corner of Highland and

Spencer M. Collins IV

Hollywood Boulevards, looking at this larger than life street mural that reads "ALL BLACK LIVES MATTER." Seeing this makes me overwhelmed with pride. As I see the colors of the rainbow that represent me as the same gender-loving black male combined with the already well-known color of BLM campaign, I'm blown away because this is the first time in history that these two entities have collaborated, and it's on such a ginormous occasion. In the past, being a part of the BLM campaign, I never felt welcomed or represented by the crowd, and witnessing the beating of a black trans woman, Iyanna Dior, only reinforced that there wasn't a space for us at this table of equality. This is why it was so important for me to be there and for the word "ALL" to be included in this declaration—to send a clear message that we are all one in this fight.

As I spoke to news reporters, the one thing I stressed was that this is just the first phase to get attention. A call to action is next, and the most important part of the day is the partnering of the two entities.

I'm so blessed to have been a part of this and to know that I indirectly was part of making it happen. The credit once again goes to Brandon and Gerald for being a YES when others wanted to say NO.

Two days after the march, I'm still on cloud nine. Being a part of that moment will forever be engraved in my spirit as one of the most significant days of my life. That's saying a lot considering all I've done in my lifetime. Something more to celebrate is the University of

Oxford Scientists investigating potential Covid-19 treatments. There is a 10-day low dose regimen of Dexamethasone that reduces the risk of death by a third for those hospitalized and on ventilators. It's not a cure, but it's the step in the right direction. and right now, we need every glimpse of hope we can get. Ten days later, the WHO announces during a virtual media briefing that they plan to deliver two billion doses of the coronavirus vaccine to people across the globe. Half of those doses will be purchased for low and middle-income countries.

I guess I missed something, because I never heard that there was a complete vaccine on the market. However, I'm happy there has been talks of one. Not sure if I'd take it if there is a vaccine, but knowing that it exists gives me a little bit of comfort.

Now that June is gone, I wonder what my 4th of July will look like with all of the social distancing restrictions? Listening to Governor Newsom, I see that bars and beaches will be restricted, and new mandates will be implemented to keep the spread of the virus down. I only hope people actually pay attention and do what's required. Health officials, concerned that the holiday celebrations may cause a spike of infections, made announcements to close down certain counties, warning that family gatherings seem to be a major source of new infections. So, we are asked not to do any gatherings where we invite folks over that are outside of the immediate family structure or household. Attending social gatherings that are outside of these restrictions directly contributes to the increase of new infections and should be canceled immediately. For those of us who have been locked away for so long, this holiday is the break we've all been waiting for, a chance to see those that we haven't been able to commune with for months. Just remember when doing so that we are still in the middle of a pandemic, and it is vital that we continue to wear our mask, wash our hands, and practice social distancing.

Being someone who recently had a small gathering and knowing how quickly we get comfortable with each other once alcohol is introduced, I pray that God keeps us all safe during this time.

Dear Governor Newsom,

I wanted to take the time to thank you for your leadership during this pandemic. Watching you reminds me of what it's like to have a well-spoken, compassionate, and caring individual in office. I only wish that #45 showed the same concern when it comes to the rest of the country and handling it with the same dignity and grace as you.

I know that there are folks that do not agree with your approach and tactics to save the city, but they are the same folks that, if given their way, would further perpetuate things beyond repair. Please continue to fight to save lives and do what's best for us during these hard and trying times, and know that not everyone is opposed to the great work you're doing to keep us safe.

Stay encouraged and mindful, and remember that being a

leader and visionary comes with a heavy burden to bear. When Noah received instructions to build the ark, folks thought he was crazy, and he was teased, ridiculed, and even mocked. As the rain came and people started to see the danger, he warned them, and they came to seek refuge. But it was too late, and they were left to drown, while those that listened and followed his instruction were saved and able to start new lives once the storm was over.

Moral of the story is: Only those that believe and take heed by following the word and instructions of God's chosen will make it to the other side of the storm where a bountiful harvest is waiting.

Grateful
Citizen Number 20201970
Spencer M Collins IV

P.S. It ain't your fault. They should've listened. PERIOD!

Chapter 8

In Conclusion of COVID

It's important as you read this last chapter to understand the purpose of this book, which is to tell and share my story so that others can do the same. I know it's not in perfect book format, and I also know that scholars will tear it apart. It's okay because I didn't write it to become a bestseller or win a Noble Peace Prize. I wrote it so people could see what the sometimes scattered mind of a depressed golden-aged, African American, HIV positive male living with Congestive Heart Failure sounds and looks like. Yes, each one of these things had an effect on me because my body doesn't work like it used to, my heart doesn't work like it used to, and my mind definitely doesn't work like it used to. It's getting harder to form and keep a thought long enough to process and capture it so that it can be shared with others. However, it is a part of my earthly assignment to do so. We all have assignments while we're here, and some live this life without ever having completed a task, while others have done so much that there is nothing left to do.

My hope is that someone will find themselves in the pages of this book and know that it's okay to feel exactly what you're feeling and most importantly, know that it's okay. Writing the book and these letters is to help us get this traumatic experience, this roller-coaster of emotions, this present time of grief, sorrow, and frustration out of our systems. There's been so much death, harm, hurt, hate, and many devastatingly life-altering events that have happened since the beginning of 2020. In the wake of it all, there are lessons that we've learned, relationships that were saved. Some that were ended, new ones that were started, old ones that were revived, and some that will never be the same.

Some of us have found ourselves, lost ourselves, discovered ourselves, even reinvented or created ourselves. We've challenged ourselves, we've healed, and even began to love ourselves. The creatives have embraced themselves in this time and have used it to make art, written series, movies, plays, songs, stories, letters, and books. We've made discoveries about ourselves and other discoveries that will shape the rest of our times here in this shared space we call Earth "HOME". Discoveries that will help some of us play a bigger game, some of us the same game, and most of us

THE COVID Letters, Vol. 1

a new game.

As I listen to the news, watch talk shows, go to appointments, meetings, fittings, readings, rehearsals, and even doctor check-ins via Skype or Zoom, one thing is apparent. Whether we decide to change or not, the world already has. Things will never be the same. I don't know if that's a good or bad thing, only that it's a matter of fact. Was our experience of the Kung-Flu/ coronavirus/COVID-19 a good and bad thing? It depends on who you ask, but for the millions infected and affected, it is a NO. For those that lost friends, family members, coworkers, and for those that have lost jobs, cars, money, and homes, it is a NO. But for those that have gained a better and deeper appreciation of life, it is a YES. So, with the bad comes some good. Was it worth it? I can't answer that. Instead, I can only say it happened, and it's still happening. That is life, and we all have to decide what we're going to do with it until our number is called and our time here expires. Use it wisely!

While you think of everything you may have lost, I also challenge you to think of everything you may have gained or accomplished. Also, be reminded that while you're doing that someone else can't because they're gone. The one thing I've taken away from this pandemic is that no one escapes deaths. We've watched as celebrities got sick, politicians, homeless, lawyers, priests, doctors, singers, children, sons, and daughters circumvented this virus. None were immune. It is by design that you're still here. So, what have you done with the time the Universe has allowed you to still exist? Even in my depression, I thank God for allowing me to still create and use my voice to help and change lives.

I could've played the victim and stayed in bed, stayed locked away, kept quiet, and protected myself from the ridicule and judgement of always choosing to be seen and heard. However, when you've been chosen to do something, you don't have a choice because it's already been made. Some of you missed that, and it's okay. I did at first, but now, I can see it clearly.

So, while you turn your nose up and shake heads criticizing what others have done, tell me how you have used this time. First, I'll start with telling you how I've used mine.

In January, I successfully transitioned from being a stage director and producer to being a television and film director.

In February, I filmed my first national campaign and shared the spotlight with my village so that they could become SAG/AFTRA eligible.

In March, I beat depression by getting outta bed and reclaiming my life.

In April, I planned a HUGE birthday celebration for the most important woman in my life, my mother, Billie Ray Collins, along with some of the most important people in my life.

Then, in May, against all odds, I turned fifty, and I'll be doing it again next year, so don't ask me any questions. When I do, just show up and say, "Happy

50th!"

In June, I was a part of something epic--the All Black Lives Matter Movement and march of solidarity between two groups that had a history of exclusion. For years, while the LGBTQI community supported BLM, it was obvious that oftentimes, our presence was not welcomed. So, I was excited when brothers, Gerald Garth of the AMAAD Institute and Brandon Anthony of B.A.S.H., helped organize this event, partnering with the organization. Not being a part of that momentous day and occasion was not an option, even though I was advised not to attend because of the possibility of mass viral infection. If I hadn't attended, I would've missed an opportunity to be a part of history. Some sacrifices are worth it, and I was willing to lose my life to defend this cause.

In July, I filmed my first full-length horror movie, and in August, I would be five years with the man who literally brings light and life into my world over and over again with his unconditional love, support, and capacity to forgive.

I know this all sounds like a big brag-fest to those who weren't listening to what this is really about. So, let me reiterate. Even though COVID has entered our lives and changed things forever, even in this darkness, there is a silver lining and a light of hope at the end of the tunnel for those looking for it. Giving up is not an option; it's a choice. I know I am bigger and more powerful than mountains of distraction sent to discourage me.

As for those of you feeling sorry for yourselves, get over it. (I'm not my diagnosis.) Come to terms with the damage you caused yourself by forgiving those who have hurt you, including yourself. Move past your hurt, pain, frustrations, and limitations to find and create bliss. I found mine in accepting me (all of me) and helping others. Find your bliss; discover what makes you happy while the world has slowed down long enough for you to figure it out. This moment is not a mistake (no moment is), because everything is created by divine design. Use this time wisely while there's still life in your body to do so. Life is too short to waste this precious time.

In the meantime, I want you to know that no matter what life throws at you, it gets better once you decide to make it happen. When you started this journey with me, it began with a little dark depression. Fear had me trapped at home and in my mind. But, now that I'm free, I'm doing auditions, readings, protests, directing, and even preparing for my first horror film as the leading man. COVID-19 is happening, people are still dying, and unfortunately, #45 is still president, but guess what? Such is life, and if you get so caught up in the scare of it all, you're going to miss it.

Wake up, be safe, and tell Miss Rona she's no longer in charge, because today, you're taking back your life.

CPSIA information can be obtained
at www.ICGtesting.com
Printed in the USA
LVHW042229061020
668072LV00004B/371